Response
– ABILITY

Paperback ISBN: 979-8-9926063-0-0
Hardcover ISBN: 979-8-9926063-1-7

Edition: First Edition

Published in Lakeville, Minnesota, by Rachel Estes Leyk.

Trigger Warning: This book contains stories that include descriptions of physical violence, which may be distressing or triggering for some readers. Please proceed with caution and prioritize your well-being while reading.

Disclaimer: The content of this book is for informational purposes only and does not constitute professional advice. The author makes no claims regarding the applicability of the information provided. Readers should consult a qualified professional for advice specific to their individual circumstances.

Cover artwork by vecteezy.com
Illustrations by Anamaria Stefan
Design & Layout by Marsha Erickson

Functions of Behavior are taken from the work of B.F. Skinner

rachelestesleyk.com / rachel@rachelestesleyk.com
Instagram: rachel_estes_leyk / LinkedIn: rachelestesleyk

Printed in the United States of America

Unleashing Awesome
Since 1975
MINNESOTA

Response
– ABILITY

How the need to unlock
a child's ability to respond
shapes the way we love,
care, support, and uplift.

—

Rachel Estes Leyk

Unleashing Awesome.
Since 1975.
MINNESOTA

Acknowledgements

This journey would not have been possible without the unwavering support, love, and encouragement of so many incredible people. To those who have walked alongside us, believed in us, and lifted us up through every challenge and victory—this book is a reflection of your impact.

A Special Thank You To:

Sean Leyk – Big Dad
Charli Estes Leyk – The Big Sister
Jennifer "Nenny" Asche – Aunt / Second Mom
Roy and Dottie Estes – Granny and Papa
Kimberly Burke – Aunt
Randy & Karen Caplinger – Great Uncle & Aunt
Mark & Patricia Estes – Great Uncle & Aunt
Jennifer Partington – Elementary Teacher
Ms. Giselle – Elementary Para
Abby Grey – 1st & 2nd Grade Teacher
Paul Helberg – Elementary Principal
David Laufenburger – 8th Grade Math Teacher / Mentor
David Swanson – 7th & 8th Grade Teacher
Sally Wattermann – Wilson Reading Tutor
Carolyn Wirkkala – 9th & 10th Grade Teacher
Amy Goetz – Attorney, School Law Center
Dr. Richard Ziegler – Neuropsychologist
Dr. Schmoe – Director & Founder of FNC

Be Joyful in hope,
Patient in affliction,
Faithful in prayer

– Romans 12:12

Foreword

Imagine sending your child to school, trusting the professionals, relying on the system, only to discover that not only is your child failing to thrive, but they are being harmed in ways no parent or caregiver should ever have to confront. This is the reality Cooper's family faced. And this book is their story, a powerful, deeply personal, and essential guide for anyone supporting a child, whether you're a parent, caregiver, or educator.

As a child neuropsychologist, I had the privilege of joining Cooper's educational journey by conducting an Independent Educational Evaluation (IEE), a comprehensive assessment performed by a professional outside the school district. These evaluations are requested when a child isn't making the expected progress in their special education program. The goal: *to better understand the child's learning, behavior, and emotional needs, and to offer clear, actionable recommendations.*

Cooper's situation was unique. A young boy with multiple medical diagnoses and autism spectrum disorder, Cooper had already faced significant challenges in school. Then came a traumatic and violent incident that further disrupted his fragile progress, adding traumatic brain injury and psychological distress to an already complex clinical picture.

When families entrust their children, especially the most vulnerable children with disabilities, to a school's special education team, they expect not just safety, but expertise, compassion, and progress. Unfortunately, Cooper's early experience exposed serious gaps in support. He was not making meaningful academic or developmental gains, and in some areas, he was regressing.

Throughout this process, one voice remained unwavering: his mother's. Her persistence, insight, and determination to advocate for her son played a critical role in reshaping his educational path. This book tells that story, not just of struggle, but of resilience and eventual success. It offers a roadmap for how collaboration can happen between families and schools, even when the terrain is difficult and emotionally charged.

What makes this book especially valuable is that it reaches far beyond the walls of a school. Cooper's mother lets us "ride along" with them during challenges and successes embedded in everyday life experiences that were often difficult for Cooper to navigate.

Cooper's mother's use of problem-solving strategies, compassion, and love provides a unique perspective that can benefit any parent and education team struggling with a child's functioning at school, home, and community.

– Dr. Richard Zielger

Richard Ziegler, PhD, LP

Dr. Richard Ziegler is a board-licensed neuropsychologist specializing in pediatric neuropsychology. He provides care for children with complex neurological and developmental conditions. His clinical expertise includes rare genetic diseases of childhood, as well as both pediatric and adult neuromuscular disorders.

Dr. Ziegler earned his PhD in Clinical Psychology with a focus in Neuropsychology from the California School of Professional Psychology and completed a fellowship in Pediatric Neuropsychology at the University of Minnesota–Twin Cities. He also has served as an Associate Professor in the Department of Pediatrics at the University of Minnesota Medical School.

v

Preface

Every journey has a defining moment, an experience that shifts perspectives, deepens understanding, and fuels a greater purpose. For me, that moment came through Cooper. It was a moment that illuminated the power of preparation, resilience, and *Response-ABILITY*, the ability to intentionally and effectively respond to challenges rather than simply react. It reinforced the importance of not only equipping those in our care with the right tools but also fostering a mindset that champions growth, advocacy, and the relentless pursuit of possibilities.

This book was born from that realization. My goal is to provide parents, caregivers, and educators with actionable strategies and frameworks to serve and support individuals in the most effective and empowering way possible. But beyond practical tools, this book is about something deeper, the mindset of advocacy and the commitment to serving others, ensuring that every child has the support they need to thrive. Advocacy is not just about overcoming obstacles; it is about embracing a vision of what is possible, even in the face of adversity. It is about choosing hope, staying steadfast, and always seeking ways to help individuals not just navigate challenges but thrive.

Cooper's story is a testament to these principles. Through his moment of resilience, I saw firsthand what it means to rise above limitations, to redefine what support looks like, and to commit fully to the growth of another. My hope is that this book serves as more than a guide; I want it to be an invitation. An invitation to reimagine how we advocate, to rethink how we support, and to reaffirm our belief in the boundless potential of those we care for.

Let's embark on this journey together.

Table of Contents

1.

Defining Moments

*When doing nothing in the moment
is doing everything right.*

"I didn't do anything."

Those were the words that shattered me.
Our son, Cooper, sat slumped in the car seat
beside me, his face streaked with tears and
marked with the cruel evidence of a brutal
lunchtime attack. His face swollen, the redness
creeping across his cheek like a dark shadow,
and his left temple throbbing from the impact

of someone else's rage. His voice cracked as he repeated himself, more to convince himself than me. "I didn't do anything."

But he had. Cooper had dared to exist.

It started like any other day, mundane and unassuming. Cooper was standing in line for lunch, chatting with a friend, a quiet smile breaking across his face as they talked about their interests in gaming. Then, out of nowhere, it began. Another boy stepped into his personal space, too close, too confrontational. Cooper, never one to tolerate being crowded, asked him to step back. A simple request. A reasonable one. The boy responded with a sneer, raising his middle finger in defiance. Cooper mirrored the gesture, a silent proclamation of boundaries.

What followed next was a cascade of misunderstandings, taunts, and fury. "Why are your hands so white?" the boy jabbed.

Cooper hesitated, puzzled by the question. He wasn't sure why his skin looked different, and for a moment, he wondered if the other boy might have an explanation. Searching for understanding rather than offense, he echoed the question back with genuine curiosity.

"I don't know. Why are your hands so black?"

His words carried no malice, only confusion, a child's attempt to make sense of something that, to him, was simply a matter of science.

But the room around them ignited as if a match had been thrown on gasoline. The boy stormed off with his friends, a volatile tide rushing to the back corner of the lunchroom. From there, they summoned someone, a student who walked with the heavy weight of his reputation, the kind of reputation that sent whispers rippling through hallways.

And that's when Cooper's nightmare began.

The boy found Cooper as he settled at a lunch table. The quiet joy of a shared meal shattered by the venomous shouts of a predator: "Say it to me! Say it to me!" Cooper barely had time to react before fists began raining down on his head, neck, and shoulders. The cafeteria erupted into chaos. Students screamed, trays clattered to the floor, and yet, the blows didn't stop. Cooper's para yelled for the attacker to stop, rushing toward him, but the boy darted away, weaving through the tables like a predator taunting its prey.

When the adults thought they'd gained control, he came back, landing punches squarely on Cooper's eye, cheek, and head. Our son didn't stand a chance. Every punch seemed to take something from him, his trust, his safety, his belief that the world could be fair. The boy struck again, this time targeting the left side of his face, the sharp crack of knuckles against skin echoing in the room as six adults tried to restrain him.

Six adults. Six people could barely contain the fury of one twelve-year old boy.

Cooper was finally whisked away to the nurse's office, trembling and silent, as the chaos in the lunchroom continued. Two hours. Two hours they waited before calling me, as if delaying the inevitable could somehow soften the blow of their failure. When the call came, my heart sank into an abyss I didn't know existed. The words didn't seem real, but the marks on Cooper's face were undeniable proof of the horror he'd endured.

When I saw him, my composure cracked like fragile glass. I tried to console him, to tell him he'd be okay, but what comfort could I offer when his trust in the world had been shattered so violently? The police officer assured us she would investigate, but her calm tone felt detached, clinical, as if this were just another routine call.

As we sat in the car, the silence between us was deafening until Cooper's voice broke through, trembling and tear-filled. "I didn't do anything."

Cooper in the car after the brutal attack

The weight of his words crushed me. He didn't do anything. He didn't provoke this. He didn't deserve this. And yet, he bore the brunt of someone else's anger, someone else's need to dominate and hurt.

I turned to him, my heart breaking at his words but my voice steady, filled with conviction. "Cooper," I said, "in not doing anything, you did everything."

He looked up at me, his swollen eyes searching my face for answers, for something to make sense of what had happened. "What do you mean?" he whispered, his voice barely audible.

"You did everything we've ever taught you," I said, my voice trembling now with the weight of emotion. "You stayed calm when chaos surrounded you. You didn't escalate the situation when you were provoked. You didn't retaliate or let anger take over. You endured one of the most stressful, life-threatening events anyone could face, and you held onto who you are. That takes courage, Cooper. That takes strength."

His tears started flowing again, but this time they carried something different, a glimmer of understanding, of validation. I reached over and placed my hand gently on him, as if willing my own strength to transfer to him.

"Think about it," I continued. "You could have fought back. You could have lashed out. But you didn't, because you knew that wasn't who you are. You stayed true to yourself, even when someone else tried to tear you down. That's what makes you strong, Cooper. That's what makes you brave."

"But it still happened," he said, his voice raw with pain. "I didn't stop it."

"No," I admitted, my voice soft but unwavering. "You couldn't stop it. Sometimes, no matter what we do, there are people who choose to hurt instead of heal, who choose anger instead of understanding. But what you did, what you *chose* to do, was not let them pull you into their storm. You stood in the middle of it, and you stayed yourself. That's everything, Cooper. That's everything we've taught you."

He nodded slowly, the tears subsiding as he

processed my words. The silence between us was thick with unspoken emotion. Then I added, "What happened to you was wrong. It should never have happened. And I promise you, Cooper, I will do everything in my power to make sure this doesn't happen again, to you or anyone else. You're not alone in this."

As we pulled into the driveway, Cooper looked at me again, his face still marked by the pain of what he'd endured but his eyes holding a spark of determination. "I didn't do anything," he said again, but this time, there was a flicker of understanding in his voice. "And that was enough."

I reached over and wrapped him in my arms, holding him tight. "It was more than enough," I said, my own tears finally falling. "It was everything."

As the evening wore on, Cooper's condition worsened, growing confusion, unbearable head pain, and his skin clammy. Without hesitation, we packed him up and rushed to the University of Minnesota Masonic Children's Hospital, the weight of uncertainty pressing down with every mile.

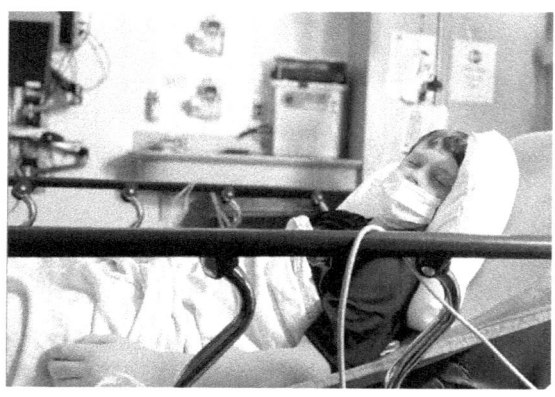

Cooper at the University of Minnesota
Masonic Children's Hospital

As I sat by Cooper's bedside in the emergency room, the harsh fluorescent lights cast an unflinching glare on the marks that marred his young face. The swelling in his face was vivid and angry, a stark reminder of the violence he'd endured. His breathing, though steady, carried the quiet rhythm of exhaustion, his small body finally succumbing to sleep despite the chaos of the day.

Leaning closer, I whispered into the stillness, my voice thick with emotion, "You are more than the worst thing that has ever happened to you, Cooper. You are resilient, brave, and so much stronger than you know. And I will always, *always* be here to remind you of that."

The steady beep of the monitors punctuated the silence, a metronome of life persisting, even in the aftermath of pain.

In the quiet darkness, I resolved to ensure that Cooper knew his worth, not just tonight, but every single day forward. He may have felt like he didn't do anything, but I knew better. He had done everything right, and I would make sure to share with others the tools Cooper called upon in that defining moment.

2.

Know it.
Own it.
Share it.

*What does my autism look like, and do I
always have to show it?*

– Cooper Estes Leyk

The sun was high in the sky, casting a golden glow on the freshly mowed soccer field where Cooper stood, feeling the unfamiliar weight of a new team's expectations. It was supposed to be a fresh start, a chance to blend his love for the game with his need for routine. But as the shouts of the new coach sliced through the air, Cooper felt the familiar tendrils of frustration and misunderstanding wrapping around him.

Cooper at Steve Michaud Park Soccer Fields

Soccer had always been Cooper's escape, a place where the order of drills and the predictability of the game's flow gave him unspeakable joy. Yet, the rhythm was off, the shouts too sharp, the glances too quick, and Cooper's ability to regulate his emotions was slipping through his fingers like sand. He knew he needed a moment, a breath, a break from the relentless tide of instructions that he couldn't seem to follow no matter how hard he tried.

So, he stepped away, placing distance between himself and the chaos, a solitary figure against the green expanse. His retreat was his silent cry for understanding, a plea for patience. But the coach, a figure of authority and discipline, saw not a child in need but a defiant player. With strides that seemed to shake the very earth, he approached Cooper, his voice climbing to a crescendo of frustration, demanding Cooper's attention, his compliance, his immediate return to the fray.

But Cooper, lost in the chaos of his own inner workings, could only stare at the ground, wishing it would swallow him whole. The silence that hung between them was a chasm, filled with unspoken words and unseen struggles. To the coach, it was disrespect; to Cooper, it was survival.

The moment shattered with the sharp crack of the soccer ball being punted across the field, a missile of anger launched by the coach's foot. It was followed by a barrage of words aimed directly at Cooper, who, with every shout, shrunk a little more into himself. "Look at me when I'm speaking to you" the coach thundered, his face the color of the evening sky, not understanding that for Cooper, this was not a simple act of looking up but a herculean task when every fiber of his being was on edge.

And there it was, the all-too-familiar dance of misunderstanding that Cooper knew too well. The frustration that simmered beneath his skin was a mirror to the coach's own, two sides of a coin, spinning endlessly in the air. But where the coach saw defiance, Cooper felt desperation; where the coach demanded action, Cooper sought support. And in the widening gap, the truth of Cooper's world lay silent and unseen, waiting for the day when understanding would bridge the divide.

The soccer field was a blur of green and the hum of energy as Cooper darted towards me, his small frame shaking with a mix of exertion and emotion. His eyes, usually so full of determination and joy on the field, were now clouded with distress, tears carving paths down his cheeks.

With his arms wrapped around me, seeking comfort and understanding, Cooper's voice trembled as he implored me to be his advocate, his interpreter to a world that so often misread his silence for defiance. "Please, tell the coach I'm autistic," he whispered between sobs, his plea a tender echo in the midst of the field's frenzy. It was a moment of heartbreak, watching my child struggle to articulate his needs in a world that wasn't designed for him.

I nodded, wrapping my arm around his shoulders, feeling the weight of his trust on my own. Together, we approached the coach, who was still untangling his own frustration, unaware of the unfolding story before him. I could feel Cooper's grip tighten, his presence a silent testament to the strength it took to stand before us, misunderstood and misrepresented.

I began to speak, words flowing in a steady stream, explaining Cooper's autism with a delicate balance of urgency and clarity. The importance of this conversation was not lost on me; I was not just explaining my son's behavior, I was educating another on the intricacies of his world. I spoke of triggers and signs, of patience and pauses, of the quiet courage that underpinned Cooper's every action on the field.

The coach's expression shifted as understanding began to dawn upon him. The stern lines of confusion softened as the narrative of Cooper's challenges and triumphs unfolded. There, in the space between misunderstanding and awareness, a bridge was slowly being built. The coach knelt down, his eyes now level with Cooper's, and in a tone that carried a newfound respect, he promised to learn, to adapt, and to support.

As we walked back to the field, I could feel the subtle shift in Cooper's demeanor. His steps were lighter, his tears had ceased, and there was a small but significant reclaiming of his love for the game. It was a small victory in the grand scheme, but for Cooper, it was a giant leap towards a world where his autism was not a barrier but a part of his unique player's profile.

Know It.

We arrived at our appointment with Dr. Richard Ziegler, prepared to start Cooper's evaluation. After checking in, we sat in the waiting room, the hum of the white noise and other families checking in for their appointments. Then, unexpectedly, Dr. Ziegler appeared in the lobby. His kind yet serious demeanor caught my attention immediately. "Can I speak with you for just a quick minute?" he asked, gesturing toward one of the consultation rooms.

Curious but slightly anxious, I followed him to the room. He closed the door softly behind us and turned to me, his expression thoughtful. "Does Cooper know he is autistic?" he asked.

The question landed like a jolt. My face must have betrayed my surprise because Dr. Ziegler immediately clarified, "I ask because some of my patients, children I've worked with, don't know. Their parents haven't told them about their diagnosis."

I paused, trying to process his words, and then responded, perhaps a bit too sharply, "Of course he knows. Why wouldn't he?"

Dr. Ziegler nodded, a gentle understanding in his eyes. "You'd be surprised. Many parents are hesitant. Some think their child won't understand. Others fear it will limit how their child sees themselves. But from what I've seen, children who understand their diagnosis, and how to work with it, are empowered. They grow stronger."

His words lingered as I reflected on our approach with Cooper. At just seven years old, he had already faced more than most adults. Along with his autism diagnosis, Cooper had been navigating life with other medical diagnoses. We had never shied away from these realities. From an early age, we believed Cooper needed to understand both his medical condition and his autism. To us, knowledge wasn't a burden, it was a gift, a tool he could use to advocate for himself and thrive in the world.

When we first explained autism to Cooper, it was a gentle conversation, woven into the fabric of our everyday life. We told him about his incredible mind, how it worked differently, how it made him uniquely Cooper. "Your brain sees patterns other people don't," I remember saying. "It's like a superpower, but sometimes, it can make certain things harder. That's why we're here to learn and grow together."

Dr. Ziegler's question reminded me how significant those conversations were, not just for Cooper, but for us as a family. Autism wasn't something to hide or fear. It was part of who Cooper was, just like his love for fire trucks or his amazing athletic ability. And while the challenges were real, so were the gifts. The spectrum, we learned, was as broad as life itself, full of color, complexity, and infinite possibility.

As I shared this perspective with Dr. Ziegler, he nodded, his face softening into a smile. "That's exactly the kind of foundation he needs," he said. "Knowing who he is will help him face whatever comes next."

That moment stayed with me, a poignant reminder of the journey we'd chosen. From the beginning, our mission wasn't just to understand autism, it was to equip Cooper with the tools to embrace it. It meant learning alongside him, celebrating his victories, and showing him how to grow through the challenges. We read books, attended workshops, and leaned on experts like Dr. Ziegler. But more than anything, we listened to Cooper. We let him teach us what he needed, what worked for him, and what didn't.

That day, I left Dr. Ziegler's office with a renewed sense of purpose. Cooper's story wasn't just ours to tell, it was his to live. And every step of the way, we would make sure he knew the truth: that he was more than his diagnosis. He was resilient, brilliant, and utterly extraordinary.

Own It.

One crisp evening, as we drove home from one of Cooper's high school soccer games, the car was filled with the afterglow of his team's victory and the rhythmic hum of the engine.

Cooper, usually reflective after his games, turned to me with a question that caught me off guard. "What does my autism look like, and do I always have to show it?" he asked, his voice tinged with curiosity and a hint of vulnerability. It was a profound question, one that opened the door to a conversation as meaningful as it was necessary.

As we navigated the traffic filled roads back home, our discussion delved into the nuances of his autism. I explained how it manifested in the way he communicated with people he wasn't familiar with, his cautious approach and the limited use of words. We talked about how he handled his emotions in stressful situations, how he had learned to identify his feelings and the strategies he used to regulate them. And then there was his relationship with humor, particularly jokes, which often puzzled him due to his literal interpretation of language.

This drive became a journey of self-discovery for Cooper. As he listened and reflected, I could see the gears turning in his mind. It was a moment of revelation for him, understanding that his autism was not just a static part of his identity but something dynamic, something that he had the power to navigate and present to the world in his own way. This realization seemed to empower him, providing a new lens through which he could view himself and his interactions with others.

The conversation illuminated for both of us how autism is not a one-size-fits-all experience. It showed Cooper that while certain traits were a part of him, they did not define him in their entirety. He began to understand that he had agency over how he engaged with the world and that his autism, though integral to his identity, was just one of the many facets that made him who he was.

As we pulled into the driveway, the car's headlights casting a warm glow on our home, there was a sense of understanding and acceptance that filled the space between us. Cooper had stepped into a new level of self-awareness, recognizing his spectrum and embracing the control he had over how he presented it to the world. It was a significant step in his journey, one that marked not just a deeper understanding of his autism but also a growing maturity in how he viewed himself and his place in the world.

Share It.

We speak openly about autism, using words that echo acceptance and understanding rather than difference and difficulty.

In the heart of our home, at a computer screen glowing against the dim light of early evening, we crafted a presentation that felt as much a part of us as our own breath. It was a PowerPoint, but not the kind filled with dry statistics or quarterly reports. This one was about Cooper, our son, with his array of challenges and his collection of strengths, all nestled within the vast universe of the autism spectrum. Slide by slide, we translated the complexities of his world into a language that others could understand and embrace.

Each slide was carefully designed to capture an aspect of Cooper's experience with autism. We used clear, concise language to articulate his sensory sensitivities, like how the buzz from a student packed lunch room could be as jarring to him as a siren. We highlighted his abilities, like his remarkable memory for facts and his love for patterns, with illustrative anecdotes and pictures. This was our olive branch to the people in his life, an invitation to see the world through Cooper's eyes.

We shared this labor of love with those who played integral roles in Cooper's daily life, his teachers, paras, and coaches. They were the conductors of his day-to-day symphony, and we believed that with this tool, they could make every note resonate in harmony with Cooper's needs and abilities. The goal was simple: to equip them with the knowledge to support Cooper, to foster an environment where he could thrive, learn, and just be a kid, without the shadow of misunderstanding darkening his path.

This proactive approach was born out of sheer necessity, forged in the face of countless struggles within the educational world. Time and time again, we encountered teachers and administrators who didn't know how to work with an autistic child. Some were willing to learn, but others revealed an unsettling lack of understanding. One administrator, in a moment that still stings, boldly asked us, "How do we teach Cooper to be normal?"

That question ignited a fire within us. "What is normal?" we shot back, our voices firm with conviction. "Who says we want Cooper to *be normal*? Our goal is not to force him into a mold dictated by societal expectations, but to accept him as he is, uniquely and beautifully himself, while helping him develop the skills he needs to navigate life."

We had already experienced the sting of misunderstandings in settings like the soccer field, where good intentions often clashed with a lack of awareness. Those moments, painful as they were, strengthened our resolve. We realized that silence wasn't an option. Cooper's needs wouldn't be met if we simply accepted the status quo or allowed ignorance to persist. Instead, we leaned into openness and education, determined to help the people in Cooper's life understand and embrace his unique way of learning and experiencing the world.

By sharing our insights, we aimed to foster
collaboration, painting a vision of a team
where every challenge was approached
with creativity and tailored strategies, and
where Cooper's strengths were not just
acknowledged, but celebrated and cultivated.
It wasn't about making Cooper fit into
their world; it was about building a bridge
of understanding so that the educational
environment could truly support him.
Each meeting, each conversation, and each
passionate response became part of a larger
mission to help those around Cooper see that
his value wasn't in conforming to a standard,
but in embracing his extraordinary potential.

Over the years, this PowerPoint evolved, just as
Cooper did. It became richer with every new
discovery, every milestone reached, and every
hurdle overcome. We gathered tips from
therapists, insights from our very own
trial & error as we walked the path, and,
most importantly, we listened to Cooper,

incorporating his feedback and respecting his growing self-awareness. It was a living document, a testament to a journey that was neither straight nor narrow, but winding and wondrous in its own right.

The act of sharing this document became a ritual of sorts, a rite of passage as each new academic year rolled around or a new season of soccer began. It was our way of extending a hand, of building a bridge before the first signs of a gap could appear. And as Cooper grew, he too began to take part in this exchange, his voice joining ours in a chorus of advocacy and understanding. It was no longer just our story to tell; it was Cooper's playbook, unfolding beautifully before us all.

Appendix Item 1 provides a content outline we utilized to organize the information, ensuring we covered all the crucial details about Cooper and his autism diagnosis.

3.

Putting Cooper at the Center

"You've understood Cooper's needs and adapted to create an environment so Cooper could thrive."

– Dr. Ruth, Psychologist from Fraser

From the moment Cooper entered our lives, with his wide-eyed gaze and gentle soul, we knew our journey with him would be one of learning, adaptation, and profound love. As a child, Cooper's world was vibrant yet complex, filled with nuances that were uniquely his own. When autism became a part of our vocabulary, it wasn't just a diagnosis; it became a lens through which we learned to see the world from Cooper's perspective. It was a path that led us not only to challenges but also to discoveries about strength, resilience, and the power of understanding.

Our search for support and resources led us to Fraser, the premier provider of autism, mental and behavioral health, and disability care. Fraser became more than just a place for services, it was a lifeline, offering expert guidance and unwavering support as we navigated the complexities of Cooper's needs. It was there that we met Dr. Ruth.

Dr. Ruth from Fraser, a beacon of guidance in our journey, remarked on our intuition and willingness to adapt. She noticed how we observed Cooper's interactions with the world, taking note of the environments where he flourished and the ones where he struggled. Her words, affirming our efforts, were a reminder of the responsibility we bore:

'to create a space where Cooper could not just exist, but thrive'.

Armed with this understanding, we began to curate a world around Cooper that was both a comfort and a catalyst for growth. We learned that routine and predictability were more than just preferences for him; they were anchors in a sea of sensory overload. So, we built a daily rhythm that Cooper could rely on, a predictable ebb and flow that soothed his worries and gave him the confidence to explore his capabilities.

But our efforts extended beyond the walls of our home. In the quaint warmth of a third-grade classroom, filled with the murmur of young voices and the occasional scrape of a chair, Cooper sat with a pencil in hand, intently gazing at a worksheet. The assignment was simple yet introspective: complete a one-page worksheet that delved into self-reflection. It asked for five words to describe oneself, a self-portrait, and a finishing statement: "One thing you need to know about me." This worksheet, seemingly straightforward, unfolded into a profound revelation for us as Cooper's parents, about how he viewed himself and how we could best nurture his self-perception.

The first task was to find five words that best described him. He carefully wrote down 'Smart,' 'Kind,' 'Silly,' 'Funny,' and 'Athletic'. Each word was a window into how he saw himself, intelligent, compassionate towards others, playful, humorous, and as someone who was athletically gifted. This insight was invaluable to us; it highlighted the blend of self-awareness and simplicity with which Cooper navigated his world.

Next, Cooper drew his self-portrait. With deliberate strokes, he sketched a figure with a wide smile and bright, curious eyes. The drawing was more than a child's artwork; it was a representation of Cooper, a visual narrative of his identity.

The last section of the worksheet, titled "One thing you need to know about me," offered the most profound insight. Cooper wrote in clear, careful letters, "I'm awesome". This concise yet impactful declaration was a window into his self-perception and how he navigated his surroundings. It highlighted his confidence and self-assuredness, while also subtly hinting at his desire for others to recognize and appreciate his unique approach to learning and engaging with the world.

When Cooper brought the completed worksheet home, it was a moment of revelation for us. We saw the clarity with which he viewed himself, and it provided us with a roadmap to support his journey of self-discovery and growth. We recognized the importance of nurturing his curiosity, of creating environments where he felt comfortable to express his friendliness, and of acknowledging and respecting his unique way of experiencing the world.

This exercise in self-reflection also reinforced our commitment to celebrate his strengths and gently guide him through his challenges. We understood that supporting Cooper wasn't just about providing him with what we thought he needed; it was about listening to his voice, understanding his perspective, and empowering him to embrace who he was and who he would become.

Cooper's third-grade worksheet became more than just a school assignment; it was a poignant reminder of the depth and complexity of a child's self-perception. It taught us that sometimes, the most profound insights come from simple questions and that by paying attention to these reflections, we can provide children with the understanding and support they need to flourish in their own unique ways.

Appendix Item 2 includes the "One Thing About Me" worksheet template.

4.

It Takes A Team

Partnering with Those
Who Lift Your Child Up

Cooper's journey has been anything but
simple. Over the years, he has faced unique
challenges that required a strong support
system, people who truly understand him,
advocate for him, and walk alongside him
through the highs and lows. Because of his
various needs and experiences, we have
learned how to quickly determine who will be
a positive force in his life. Some people come
and go, while others become pillars of support,
shaping his growth in ways we never expected.

One of those pillars is Mr. Laufenburger, Cooper's 8th-grade math teacher.

After the lunchtime assault, Cooper was left not only with physical injuries but also emotional scars. The school environment that once felt familiar had become a place of fear, making it clear that a change was necessary for his well-being. Leaving behind friends, routines, and a sense of stability was not easy, but we knew that finding a new school where he felt safe and supported was the best choice.

Naturally, Cooper was on edge about entering an unfamiliar setting, especially one that had limited experience working with students on the autism spectrum. The transition was made even harder by the trauma he had endured, compounding his concerns about whether his new school would truly understand and support his needs. The unfamiliarity made an already tough transition even harder. But amidst the uncertainty, Cooper found an unexpected ally in Mr. Laufenburger.

From the beginning, Cooper formed a quick connection with his math teacher. As with any trusted adult in his life, he had to test the waters first. Pushing buttons was Cooper's way of assessing trust. Seeing how someone would react, gauging whether they were truly invested or if they would give up on him at the first sign of difficulty. Time and time again, Mr. Laufenburger showed up in a way that built trust, even on Cooper's worst days. Instead of frustration, he met Cooper's challenges with patience, humor, and an unwavering commitment to their relationship.

One of my favorite memories of Cooper testing Mr. Laufenburger happened when Cooper blurted out in class, "This class sucks!" The room fell silent as every student turned to see what would happen next. Mr. Laufenburger took a moment, carefully considering his response. Then, with a straight face, he said, "You know what else sucks? The fact that I had beans for lunch and later I'll be filling this room with my farts." The tension instantly broke as

Cooper and the entire class burst into laughter. That simple moment of humor not only diffused the situation but also reinforced the trust and connection Cooper had with his teacher.

I remember meeting Mr. Laufenburger for the first time and asking him what motivated him to handle Cooper the way he did. His response was simple yet profound. He said he had two choices when interacting with students like Cooper, he could engage in a power struggle, or he could lean into the moment and create laughter. He always chose laughter. That choice alone transformed Cooper's engagement and participation in ways we hadn't seen before. It wasn't just about getting through a math lesson; it was about forming a connection that made learning possible.

At the end of 8th grade, Mr. Laufenburger told me something I'll never forget. He said he was "one of Cooper's people." He shared his philosophy that every child needs at least five trusted adults in their lives in addition to their parents. He made it clear that he intended to be one of those five for Cooper. True to his word, now that Cooper is in 11th grade, Mr. Laufenburger still checks in with him—and with us. He has made it a point to be present at Cooper's soccer game, cheering him on from the sidelines, just as Cooper has shown his support by attending a volleyball game that Mr. Laufenburger coached.

Cooper with Mr. David Laufenburger after a High School Soccer Game

He continues to advocate for Cooper, working with his peer educators and offering insightful tips on how to engage with him for optimal participation. His presence is a reminder that the right people make all the difference in a child's journey.

Through Cooper's experience, we've gathered some key insights about building a strong support team.

Know who you need and why you need them.

Not every person will be the right fit. Identify those who bring essential skills, expertise, or emotional support that align with your child's needs, whether it's a therapist for emotional growth, a teacher for academic success, a coach for confidence-building, or an advocate to navigate complex systems.

Ensure they lead with their heart.

The best team members are those who show up with compassion and commitment rather than just obligation. You can recognize these individuals by the way they listen attentively, adapt to challenges with patience, and consistently seek to uplift and empower your child. They don't just perform a role, they genuinely invest in building a meaningful connection, demonstrating empathy, and showing a willingness to learn and grow alongside your child.

Be open to new people joining the team.

Each stage, childhood, adolescence, or early adulthood, brings its own complexities. As your child grows, their needs will evolve, requiring new expertise and support along the way. This may mean introducing a specialized therapist during periods of heightened anxiety, finding a mentor to foster social development, or engaging an academic coach to navigate new educational challenges. As these changes arise, assembling a team with fresh perspectives and tailored strategies becomes essential to meeting your child's evolving needs.

Leverage their voices in difficult conversations.

Sometimes, having other trusted adults advocate on your child's behalf can make all the difference when dealing with those who don't understand their needs. This can look like a teacher explaining how specific learning strategies work best for your child, a coach highlighting their strengths and potential, or a therapist providing insight into emotional or behavioral challenges. These voices can validate your child's experience, bridge gaps in understanding, and create a more supportive environment by influencing decision-makers in schools, sports, or other settings.

Express gratitude often and always.

Genuine appreciation goes a long way in ensuring that those who stand by your child know how much they are valued. This could be as simple as a heartfelt thank-you note, acknowledging their impact in a conversation, or finding meaningful ways to give back to them. Gratitude strengthens relationships and reinforces the bond between your child and their support system, encouraging them to continue investing their time and energy. When people feel recognized and appreciated, they are more likely to remain engaged and committed to helping your child thrive.

Having a team means never facing challenges alone. It means knowing that when things get tough, there are people who will stand by your child, advocate for them, and help them navigate the world. Cooper's journey has shown us time and time again that the right people, with the right heart and the right approach, can make all the difference.

5.

The Response - **ABILITY** Toolbox

The child-centered framework three essential pillars:
Advocate, Motivate, and Participate

In the intricate tapestry of parenting, especially for children with unique needs, adopting a framework that positions your child at the center is pivotal. This approach is not just about providing support; it's about empowering them with the right tools and skills to navigate their world. This framework is built on three foundational pillars: advocate, motivate, and participate. Each pillar plays a crucial role in the comprehensive growth of the child, ensuring they are equipped to face the world with confidence and resilience.

The first pillar, 'Advocate' emphasizes the importance of knowledge, support, awareness, and acceptance. This involves educating the child about their own strengths and challenges, helping them to develop a deeper understanding of themselves. It's about fostering a sense of self-awareness that enables them to articulate their needs and seek support when necessary. Advocacy also extends to the parents and caregivers, who must advocate for the child's needs in various settings, be it at school, in social gatherings, or within the family. This pillar is crucial in building a child's confidence to stand up for themselves and seek understanding and support from others.

The second pillar, 'Motivate,' is centered around fostering a positive mindset and attitude in the child. This involves setting achievable goals and tying them to meaningful rewards. It's about helping the child see the value in their efforts, regardless of the outcome. For instance, if a child struggles with social interactions, setting a goal to initiate a conversation and tying it to a reward that resonates with them can be motivating. It's about creating a learning environment that is driven by encouragement and recognition, where each step forward, no matter how small, is celebrated.

The final pillar, 'Participate,' focuses on understanding and managing triggers and responses, as well as optimizing the environment and sensory experiences. This is particularly crucial for children who may be sensitive to sensory inputs or certain social scenarios. By identifying what triggers challenging behaviors or emotional responses, parents can preemptively create strategies to address them. This might involve modifying the learning environment to reduce sensory overload or practicing response strategies in a safe, supportive setting. Participation is not just about being present; it's about being engaged in a way that respects the child's unique needs and preferences.

Adding to the framework of putting the child at the center and surrounding them with the pillars of Advocate, Motivate, and Participate, it's crucial to recognize the foundational elements these pillars enhance, particularly in the areas of social, emotional, and communication capabilities. These elements are not just supplementary; they are integral to the child's overall development and well-being.

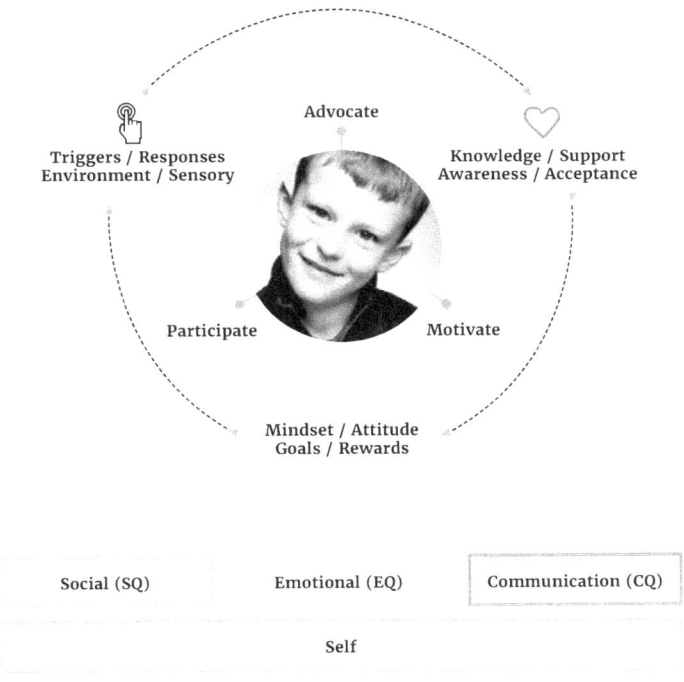

Communication is another critical area enhanced by these pillars. The 'Advocate' pillar, in particular, emphasizes the development of self-advocacy skills, a key aspect of communication. As children learn about their strengths and challenges, they become better equipped to communicate their needs and seek support. This knowledge empowers them to articulate their thoughts and feelings more effectively, fostering better communication with parents, teachers, and peers. Additionally, the motivation to engage in social settings and the participation in environments tailored to their needs further refine their communication skills, making them more effective and confident communicators.

In the realm of social capabilities, the 'Motivate' pillar plays a pivotal role. By encouraging a positive mindset and setting attainable goals, children are more inclined to engage socially. They learn to associate social interactions with positive outcomes, whether it's through the achievement of goals or the rewards that follow. This motivation extends to participating in group activities or initiating interactions, which are vital components of social development. Moreover, the 'Participate'' pillar helps children navigate social environments by teaching them to recognize and manage triggers, thereby reducing social anxiety and enhancing their ability to engage with peers.

Emotionally, these pillars foster resilience and self-awareness. The process of setting and achieving goals under the 'Motivate' pillar strengthens emotional resilience, teaching children that they can overcome challenges and achieve success. The 'Participate' pillar, with its focus on understanding environmental and sensory inputs, allows children to become more attuned to their emotional responses and develop strategies to manage them. This awareness is crucial in emotional regulation and developing a sense of control over one's emotional state.

Each of these foundational elements, social, emotional, and communication capabilities, are interwoven and mutually reinforcing. The growth in one area can catalyze development in others. For instance, enhanced communication skills can lead to more meaningful social interactions, which in turn can improve emotional well-being. Similarly, emotional resilience can foster a more positive mindset, fueling motivation and participation.

By adopting a child-centered approach and emphasizing the pillars of Advocate, Motivate, and Participate, parents and caregivers play a pivotal role in enhancing their child's social, emotional, and communication capabilities. This holistic strategy goes beyond addressing specific challenges to foster comprehensive growth and development, arming the child with the necessary skills and confidence for effective world navigation. This framework is designed to evolve with each child's unique journey, adapting to their growth, challenges, and ever-changing needs. As parents guide their children through the intricacies of these pillars, they do more than just lead; they learn and grow alongside them, forging a relationship based on mutual respect, understanding, and unwavering support.

This approach goes beyond the conventional methodologies of parenting. It's about creating a nurturing ecosystem where the child feels seen, heard, and valued. It's a commitment to walking hand-in-hand with the child through their journey of growth and discovery, helping them to unlock their potential in a world that is learning to embrace diversity in all its forms.

Core Competencies Capabilities Map

Social (SQ)		Emotional (EQ)		Communication (CQ)	
Social Awareness	Relationship Management	Emotional Awareness	Emotional Management	Intrapersonal	Interpersonal
Social Standards/ Principles	Interpersonal Skills	Emotional Identification	Response Management	Speech Development	Advocacy Management
Situational Awareness	Conflict Management	Emotional Regulation	Choice Management	Self-Reflection Management	Response Management
Situational Management	Skill Management	Classification Management	Action Management	Response Methods	Eye Contact Management
Bias Management	Decision Making	Trigger Points	Maturity Management	Self Talk	Listening Skills
Impact Management	Communication Management	Temperament	Impulse Management	Perception Management	Verbal/ Non-Verbal Management
Trigger Management	Trust Building			Expectation Management	Feedback Management

Self

Self Awareness	Self Management
Diagnosis Awareness	Outcomes Management
Self-Worth	Mindset Management
Self-Confidence	Default Settings
Sensory Awareness	Guiding Principles
Trigger Points	Coping Tool Management
Value Identification Management	Stress Management
Environmental Management	

Toolbox

Navigating the journey of building social, emotional, and communication capabilities in a child, especially one as unique as Cooper, requires a toolbox of strategies, some standard and some innovatively crafted. Over time, in working closely with Cooper, we have developed and fine-tuned a set of tools that have become indispensable in his growth. These tools, now part of Cooper's personal playbook, have been pivotal in guiding his interactions and responses in various situations, most notably the lunchtime attack, shaping his understanding of himself and the world around him.

We will provide a high-level overview of the seven core tools that make up this toolbox, each one designed to support key aspects of a child's development, from emotional regulation to self-advocacy and effective communication. These tools were not created overnight; they were shaped through experience, trial and error, and continuous refinement to ensure they evolved with Cooper's unique journey.

This overview will offer insight into how each tool functions and the role it plays in fostering growth and resilience. Then, in the following seven sections, we will dive deeper into each tool individually, breaking down its purpose, practical application, and real-world impact. By the end, you'll have a clear understanding of not just what these tools are, but how they can be adapted and implemented to support any child in navigating their own path to success.

One fundamental tool is understanding the functions of behavior, which include attention seeking, tangible, avoidance, and sensory. By recognizing what drives Cooper's behaviors, we have been able to address them with appropriate solutions, effectively setting what we refer to as his "Default Settings". This understanding helps in preemptively managing situations, ensuring that Cooper's responses are more in line with the expectations and norms of his environment.

Another key strategy is 'Odd or Even,' a simple yet effective way of instilling flexibility in daily life. This approach allows Cooper, and others in the family, to have their choice in certain situations, fostering a sense of fairness and balance. It's a tool that not only aids Cooper in adapting to change but also ensures that other family members feel included and valued.

'Stretch Yourself' is a goal-setting tool that encourages Cooper to be aware of the efforts needed to stay in what we call the 'green zone', a state of calm and control. This strategy, symbolized by the stretching of a rubber band, involves reflecting on the day's events to learn and improve. It's about recognizing that every day is a new opportunity to grow and show up better.

We also focus on living by moments, a mindset that emphasizes celebrating all victories, even the smaller ones. This philosophy teaches Cooper that his worth is not defined by challenging moments. It involves storytelling, where we use real-life situations to extract valuable life lessons; helping Cooper navigate his emotions and responses. Phrases like "Okay, I am Cooper and I..." become starting points for these stories, allowing him to explore different scenarios and outcomes.

'Two-One-None' is another technique that highlights the power of disengaging from conflict. It's based on the principle that it takes two to argue, so if one person drops out, there is no argument.

Similarly, 'Never be Player B' focuses on the strength of disengaging with silence, reinforcing the idea that one doesn't get into trouble for remaining silent.

Lastly, 'Scaled Responses' is a tool that helps Cooper gauge the magnitude of his reactions. It's about matching the response to the size of the problem, small problems warrant small responses, and big problems call for more significant responses. This tool is crucial in helping him navigate emotional regulation and response proportionality.

Together, these tools form a comprehensive framework that guides through the complexities of social interactions, emotional regulation, and effective communication. They are not just strategies but life skills that empower Cooper to navigate his world with more confidence and resilience, setting the foundation for a future where he can continue to grow and thrive.

5. A

Functions of Behavior

Know what drives the behaviors and address them with the right solution approaches

When Cooper was three years old, our days were punctuated by a curious and repetitive dance with his shoes. Each morning, we would gently slip them onto his tiny feet, only to find them discarded moments later. This cycle repeated itself tirelessly, leaving us perplexed and, admittedly, a bit frustrated. His small hands would work diligently to remove the shoes, his determination unwavering, all while telling us, "They are buzzing me!" We couldn't understand what drove this behavior; it seemed like a harmless quirk of childhood at first.

However, this wasn't the only puzzle we faced with Cooper. When he yearned for our attention and didn't receive it immediately, he would erupt into a meltdown. These emotional outbursts were intense and, as first-time parents of an autistic child, we felt lost in a sea of uncertainty about how to respond effectively. We wondered if these were just typical toddler behaviors or signs of something we were yet to understand. It was a time of quiet desperation, feeling like we were missing a crucial piece of the parenting puzzle.

Our breakthrough came when Fraser introduced us to the concept of the Four Functions of Behavior. This framework was a revelation, shedding light on the fact that all behavior, even in someone as young as Cooper, has a purpose, a function that we had previously been unaware of. We learned that behaviors could be a means of seeking attention, accessing something tangible, avoiding a disliked situation, and/or responding to sensory needs.

Armed with this new understanding, we began to see Cooper's actions in a different light. His insistence on removing his shoes wasn't mere child's play or stubbornness; it was a form of communication, a way of responding to a sensory need or perhaps even seeking our attention. The meltdowns when he felt ignored were not just tantrums; they were his way of expressing a need for interaction, a tangible response to the lack of attention he was experiencing.

This knowledge transformed our approach to parenting. We became more observant, learning to read the subtle cues behind Cooper's behaviors. Instead of simply putting his shoes back on repeatedly, we started to explore different types of footwear, considering sensory-friendly options, and creating routines that included Cooper in the process, making it a game rather than a chore. Regarding his need for attention, we found ways to proactively engage with him, ensuring he felt seen and heard, even before a meltdown could occur. Understanding the Four Functions of Behavior didn't just provide us with strategies; it gave us empathy and insight into Cooper's world. Our parenting decisions became more informed and effective, not because we had all the answers, but because we had learned to listen to Cooper's unique way of communicating his needs. This journey with Cooper, albeit challenging, was enriching, teaching us that sometimes, the most profound lessons in parenting come from understanding the silent language of behavior.

The concept of the functions of behavior, a cornerstone in understanding human actions, particularly in the field of Applied Behavior Analysis (ABA), is largely attributed to the work of B.F. Skinner, a renowned psychologist and behaviorist. Skinner's groundbreaking research and theories in the mid-20th century laid the foundation for identifying and categorizing behaviors based on their functions. His work emphasized the idea that behaviors are not random but are purposeful actions driven by specific motivations or needs. The classification of behaviors into categories such as seeking attention, escaping or avoiding undesired situations, accessing tangible items, and/or fulfilling sensory needs, are deeply rooted in Skinner's behaviorist theories. These concepts have since been expanded and refined by numerous behavior analysts and psychologists, but the origin of understanding behavior through its function is a testament to Skinner's pioneering contributions to behavioral psychology.

Below, we will take a closer look at these

functions of behavior, how they have manifested in Cooper's life, and the supportive responses we have implemented to align with each function, helping him navigate challenges more effectively and thrive in his daily experiences.

Attention-Seeking

Attention-seeking behaviors often manifest when an individual, especially a child, engages in actions aimed at eliciting a response or feedback from others. These behaviors can vary widely, from vocal expressions like yelling, crying, or interrupting, to physical actions such as tapping repeatedly on a surface or acting out disruptively in a classroom setting. At the heart of these behaviors lies a fundamental need for recognition, interaction, and validation. Whether the individual is seeking eye contact, a verbal acknowledgment, or simply the assurance of another person's presence, the behaviors are not random, they are a form of communication. They express a deep desire for connection and a way of saying, "I need to know that I matter to you."

One of the most effective tools we've found for addressing these behaviors is a simple yet powerful phrase we frequently use with Cooper: "I see you." This phrase acknowledges the need behind the behavior without reinforcing negative patterns. It communicates to the child that their presence and emotions are recognized and valued, providing the connection they seek without escalating the situation.

It's important to approach attention-seeking behaviors with empathy and understanding. While these actions can be challenging to manage, they are often a child's way of navigating their emotions and seeking assurance in their relationships. By offering recognition in a calm and consistent manner, we create opportunities to guide them toward more constructive ways of seeking attention.

Balancing the response is key. It involves validating the child's need for connection while teaching them healthier ways to express that need. With patience, consistency, and tools like verbal acknowledgment, such as "I see you.", we can turn challenging moments into opportunities for growth, helping the child develop a stronger sense of security and self-worth.

Situation	Trigger(s)	Behavior(s)	Supportive Response
Dog Sitter came to house to get instructions and house keys	– Talking – New Person in Space – Mom occupied visiting with someone	– Jumping/ running around the house – Being extra loud	– Acknowledge "I see you" – Incorporate – Assign task

Escape / Avoidance

Cooper has always approached homework with the same level of enthusiasm one might have for cleaning out the garage on a sweltering summer day, none at all. After a full day at school, his aversion to more structured tasks became a predictable yet creative routine of avoidance. His shenanigans were, at times, impressively innovative, hiding under the table, conveniently needing a snack, or suddenly discovering the dire importance of organizing his Lego collection. Each evening felt like a tug-of-war, with homework on one end of the rope and Cooper's determination to avoid it on the other.

These behaviors are a textbook example of the escape function. When faced with a task that feels overwhelming, stressful, or simply undesirable, individuals often engage in actions designed to remove themselves from the situation. Avoidance behaviors like hiding under a table to dodge homework, leaving the room during a difficult discussion, or faking an illness to skip school are all motivated by the same underlying need: to escape from an uncomfortable or challenging demand.

Understanding this motivation was key to helping Cooper navigate his struggles with homework. Instead of pulling on the rope of avoidance and escalating the tension, I chose to remain flexible in my approach. I realized that forcing him into compliance would only make the task more daunting, reinforcing his need to escape. Instead, I focused on modifying how the work got done, adapting to his needs in the moment to make the process more manageable and less intimidating.

Sometimes, this meant letting him sit in his favorite spot on the couch instead of at the dining table. Other times, it involved breaking the homework into smaller, less overwhelming chunks or incorporating short breaks between tasks. I also learned to participate in ways that felt supportive rather than controlling, such as working alongside him or offering encouragement in a calm, steady voice.

This approach didn't just help Cooper complete his assignments, it also taught him how to engage with challenging situations in a more constructive way. By showing flexibility and understanding, I was able to model coping strategies and provide the support he needed to confront his discomfort rather than flee from it. Over time, the struggle with homework became less about escape and more about finding a rhythm that worked for both of us.

Recognizing the escape function of behavior and addressing it with empathy and adaptability can make a world of difference. It's not about forcing compliance but about understanding the root cause of the behavior and creating a supportive framework. For Cooper, this meant turning homework time from a battleground into an opportunity for growth, one flexible moment at a time.

Situation	Trigger(s)	Behavior(s)	Supportive Response
Doing homework in the evening after a long day of school	– Facing into challenge skill areas – Working without accommodations – Self-conscious about confidence	– Delay – Excuse making – Goofing around	– Give choice of what to do first – Acknowledge "I know this is hard" or "I know this isn't your Favorite subject" – Provide modifications & Support

Access to Tangibles

Centered around the pursuit of obtaining specific physical items or rewards that an individual desires. A child may exhibit persistent pleading, crying, or even tantrums to gain access to a coveted toy, a preferred food item, or permission to engage in a desired activity like watching TV or playing video games.

The key motivation here is the acquisition of a tangible object or experience that holds value for the individual.

For years, trips to Target were a battleground rooted in accessing tangible items. Cooper would light up as soon as we entered the store, his eyes scanning the shelves filled with bright toys, games, and all the things he wanted to take home. Each item was a tangible object that promised joy and excitement.

But when the inevitable "no" came, a necessary boundary, it was like flipping a switch. The disappointment was too much, and his emotions would erupt into a full-blown meltdown. Tears, yelling, and the desperate stares of other shoppers became a regular part of these outings. Each trip ended in exhaustion, not just for Cooper but for us too, as we struggled to balance his wants with the realities of the moment. It was clear he wasn't yet equipped to handle the sensory and emotional challenges of such a trip.

Recognizing and understanding this function is crucial, as it guides the approach to managing such behaviors. It involves striking a balance between appropriately rewarding positive behavior and avoiding the reinforcement of negative behaviors, all while teaching the individual healthier ways to express their wants and negotiate for tangible rewards.

Situation	Trigger(s)	Behavior(s)	Supportive Response
Shopping at Target	– Visual of toys – Lots of stimulation in a variety of forms	– Melting down – Big voice – Negotiating	– Limit exposure to the environment – Bring Goldy our service dog – Create agreement before going in the store

Sensory Stimulation

Sensory processing differences significantly influence how individuals interact with their environment. For those with these differences, behavior often serves as a way to satisfy sensory cravings or alleviate sensory discomfort. Understanding this sensory function is critical in creating supportive environments that meet the unique needs of the individual.

For example, some individuals might engage in behaviors such as hand-flapping, rocking, or spinning objects to fulfill their need for specific sensory input. These actions can be soothing, helping them regulate their sensory environment and regain a sense of control. In other cases, individuals may avoid sensory overload by engaging in behaviors that minimize overwhelming input, such as covering their ears or seeking quiet, less stimulating spaces.

Cooper's relationship with clothing is an example of how sensory needs influence behavior. For as long as we can remember, Cooper has been highly sensitive to what he wears, especially when it comes to formal attire. The texture of dress clothes, the tightness of a collar, or even the weight of certain fabrics can become overwhelming, making events that require dressing up particularly challenging.

Over time, we've discovered that involving Cooper in the process of preparing for these events transforms the experience. By giving him advance notice and allowing him to select his own dress clothes, we empower him to feel more in control of the situation. This collaboration often led to success, as Cooper can find options that feel comfortable while meeting the dress code requirements.

One unexpected but delightful strategy has been drawing inspiration from his Big Dad's choice of outfits. *Big Dad* is Cooper's dad, a nickname the kids gave him when they were little because they said he had a big heart, though it didn't hurt that he's also a big guy. When Cooper's attire mirrors his Big Dad's, whether it's a suit, a tie, or even the choice of shoes, it creates a sense of connection and pride. This approach not only reduces his sensory discomfort but also builds his confidence and makes formal occasions more enjoyable for him.

Understanding and addressing sensory needs like Cooper's, requires empathy and thoughtful adaptation. By recognizing the sensory processing function of his behavior and providing solutions, such as advance planning, choice, and sensory-friendly options, we've been able to create a more supportive environment for him. Whether through tools like sensory-friendly spaces or personalizing experiences, these interventions allow individuals to regulate their sensory experiences in ways that promote comfort, confidence, and well-being.

Each of these sensory-based strategies reflects the broader importance of tailoring responses to meet the unique needs of the individual. By doing so, we create pathways for growth, self-regulation, and positive interactions with the world around them.

Situation	Trigger(s)	Behavior(s)	Supportive Response
The type of clothing he wears	– Certain textures – The fit being too tight – Zippers or hoods – Color – red	– Refusal to wear – Complaining – Limiting selection to only a few items	– Provide choices – Accept what works for him – Provide plenty advance notice if the attire will be outside comfort zone

Understanding these functions is crucial for interpreting and categorizing an individual's actions, as well as uncovering the underlying reasons for specific behaviors. By aligning your response with the function of the behavior, you can deliver the most effective and supportive response, ensuring a meaningful and lasting impact both now and in the future.

5. B

Odd or Εven

Creating flexibility in daily moments
while allowing others to have their choice

When Cooper was younger, car rides were often a battleground of clashing preferences. Our family car, which should have been a space of shared journeys and cheerful banter, became a zone of contention, particularly between Cooper and his sister, Charli. The root of these frequent skirmishes? Music. While Charli, our daughter, has a deep love for singing along to songs on the car radio, Cooper preferred absolute silence. He found the music and singing not just distracting, but distressingly overwhelming.

This disparity in their needs turned every car journey into a tussle of wills. Charli, ever eager to express her joy and enthusiasm through song, would often forget Cooper's aversion to music. Meanwhile, Cooper, unable to cope with the sensory overload that music presented to him, would react sharply, demanding the music be turned off. Their voices would rise, words would be exchanged, and what should have been a peaceful family drive would spiral into a storm of tears, and frustration.

This went on for over a year, with each car trip feeling like a rerun of the previous one, filled with tension and the inevitable clash between Cooper and Charli. It was a cycle of stress that seemed unending. As a parent, it pained me to see such discord between the two of them and to witness the strain it put on what should have been simple, everyday activities like driving to school or running errands.

It was then that I decided a new approach was needed, something that could balance both their needs while restoring peace during our drives. Thus, the concept of 'odd or even days' was born. The rule was simple: on even days, Charli would have the freedom to sing along to her heart's content, and on odd days, the car would remain a quiet zone, free of music, for Cooper's comfort. This method was not just about maintaining order; it was a lesson in mutual respect and understanding for their differing needs.

Determining who would be assigned 'odd' and 'even' days of the week in our new family system was surprisingly straightforward, thanks to a simple yet effective idea based on their birth months. Charli, born in an even month, naturally became our 'even' representative. Cooper, on the other hand, was born in an odd month, making him the perfect fit for the 'odd' days. This method of using their birth months as the basis for assigning 'odd' and 'even' roles provided a clear, unbiased way of dividing days between them. It was a logical decision that added a personal touch, rooting the method in something as simple as their birthdays. This approach eliminated randomness and gave each child a sense of ownership, enhancing both fairness and effectiveness.

The implementation of 'odd days' in our 'odd or even' method played a crucial role in fostering flexibility and resilience in Cooper, who often showed a preference for fixed routines and predictability due to his unique needs. On even days, when it was Charli's turn to make choices, Cooper was gently nudged out of his comfort zone. These were the days when he would need to adapt to situations that weren't always aligned with his preferences, such as listening to music in the car or watching a movie chosen by his sister.

This regular, gentle stretching of Cooper's boundaries on even days acted much like the gentle stretching of a rubber band. It created a sort of elasticity in his behavior and mindset, gradually increasing his tolerance for change and uncertainty. Over time, these experiences contributed to a subtle yet significant shift in Cooper. He began to demonstrate increased flexibility in his daily interactions and a greater openness to new experiences. The 'odd days' became more than just a turn-taking exercise; they were instrumental in helping Cooper develop coping mechanisms for dealing with changes and unpredictability.

Moreover, this routine of alternating days allowed Cooper to experience and understand the concept of compromise and sharing in a tangible way. It underscored the importance of considering others' needs and preferences, not just his own. This was particularly beneficial for his social and emotional development, as he learned to navigate and adapt to the dynamics of family life and beyond.

In essence, the 'odd day' was an invaluable tool in helping Cooper gradually move away from a fixed mindset, fostering a more adaptable and resilient approach to life's varying scenarios. This growth was a testament to the effectiveness of introducing a structured yet flexible method to help develop essential life skills.

Implementing this method brought about other significant changes. Cooper and Charli slowly began to appreciate and respect each other's preferences. Charli learned to enjoy her singing days while being considerate of Cooper's need for quiet. Cooper, on the other hand, started to understand the joy his sister derived from music and singing. The 'odd or even days' rule taught them about compromise and empathy, essential skills for navigating not just their current disagreements but future relationships and situations.

The 'odd or even days' method soon expanded beyond just regulating music in the car; it seamlessly integrated into various aspects of our daily family life, evolving into a valuable tool for decision-making and promoting fairness. Whenever a choice presented itself, be it who got to sit in the front seat during a drive, who would sit next to mom on an airplane ride, or who had the privilege of picking the movie on family movie night, the 'odd or even' rule came into play. This method not only simplified decisions but also instilled a sense of equality and turn-taking between Cooper and Charli. It taught them to anticipate and respect each other's turns, leading to fewer arguments and a more harmonious family environment. Each of them knew that their chance to make a choice was just around the corner, which helped in fostering patience and reducing conflicts. The implementation of this method in these everyday situations was a game-changer, transforming potential moments of contention into opportunities for cooperative and respectful family interactions.

5. C

Stretch Yourself

Make time to reflect on daily moments while grounding in values of fairness, kindness, and humility

Cooper's days were filled with the joys and challenges of growing up, and like any child, he sometimes struggled to stay calm and in control during stressful situations. As Cooper's parents, we were always eager to help him thrive, introducing a new strategy called "Stretch Yourself" to help him stay in what we referred to as the 'green zone', a state of calm and balance.

Every morning, on the drive to school, we discussed three key ways to show up in life: to be fair and just, to be kind and loving, and to remain humble. This simple ritual became a framework for how Cooper could navigate his day, making choices aligned with these values. At the end of each day, we reflected together, celebrating moments when he lived up to these principles and identifying opportunities to stretch and grow.

One afternoon, after a particularly chaotic day at school, I talked with Cooper on the drive home. I handed him a small rubber band and said, "This rubber band is a reminder of our new goal-setting tool. It's called 'Stretch Yourself.' Just like this band stretches, we can stretch ourselves to handle challenges better and stay in the green zone while staying fair, kind, and humble."

Curious, Cooper listened as I explained further. "Every day, we will reflect on what happened and think about how we handled different situations. We will ask ourselves: Were we fair? Were we kind? Were we humble? We will set small goals to help us improve and show up better tomorrow. Every day is a new chance to grow."

That afternoon, we began our first "Stretch Yourself" session. "How was your day, Cooper?" I asked.

Cooper sighed, thinking back to an argument he had with a friend during recess. "I got really mad when we couldn't agree on what game to play. I yelled, and we both ended up mad."

I nodded, understanding. "It's okay to feel upset, but let's think about how we can handle these situations better. Were we fair to our friend? Were we kind to each other? And did we stay humble enough to listen to one another?"

Together, we discussed different strategies. Cooper suggested taking a deep breath or walking away to cool down before talking again. We set a small goal for the next day: if a disagreement happened again, Cooper would try to stay calm and focus on fairness by suggesting a compromise.

Over the next few years, "Stretch Yourself" became a daily routine for us. We used the rubber band as a physical reminder of our values and progress. Each afternoon, we reflected on the day's events, celebrating moments of fairness, kindness, and humility, and learning from setbacks. Cooper began to see each day as an opportunity to grow, understanding that even when he didn't show up perfectly, he could always stretch himself to do better next time.

One particular day, Cooper came home beaming. "Mom, today I almost got into another argument with my friend, but I remembered our talk. I took a deep breath and asked if we could play both games, one after the other. It worked! We had a great time."

Cooper goofing around with his teacher
Mrs. Abby Grey and his best friend Jonny.

I smiled. "That's amazing, Cooper. You were
fair by suggesting a compromise, kind in how
you approached it, and humble enough to see
another perspective. I'm so proud of you."

The "Stretch Yourself" tool became a
cornerstone of Cooper's life. Through the
practice of reflection and goal-setting, he
grew more aware of his emotions and learned
practical ways to manage them while keeping

fairness, kindness, and humility at the heart of his actions. By looking through life with these guiding principles, Cooper discovered how to handle life's ups and downs with grace and resilience.

As time went on, his confidence grew. Cooper approached challenges with a mindset of growth, always striving to show up better each day. The simple act of reflecting on fairness, kindness, and humility transformed his approach to life, helping him navigate relationships and challenges with wisdom and compassion.

5. D

Live by Moments

Do not let moments define the entire day

Throughout his elementary school years, Cooper was enrolled in a before and after school care program. Like all children, Cooper experienced a mix of good days and challenging moments. Yet, he often encountered a persistent problem with how the staff perceived his behavior. Any time he faced a difficult moment, whether it involved a short-lived bout of frustration or a phase of quiet withdrawal, the care providers quickly concluded that he was having a bad day in its entirety. This judgment became so routine that it turned into the usual update I received from the staff when I arrived to pick him up after my workday.

This generalization of Cooper's behavior became a significant concern. Each incident, regardless of its scale or context, was viewed not as an isolated moment, but as a reflection of his entire day. This approach not only overlooked the nuances of Cooper's experiences but also disregarded the possibility of him recovering or turning his day around. The care providers, though well-intentioned, failed to see that a single challenging moment didn't define Cooper's entire day.

For Cooper, this was both physically and emotionally draining. He felt as though he was constantly under a microscope, where every slip-up was magnified and extended to overshadow all his positive moments and efforts. This perspective from the adults around him created a sense of helplessness and frustration. Cooper began to feel as if he was walking on eggshells, knowing that one bad moment could unfairly characterize his whole day.

In reflecting on Cooper's experience, I was reminded of Dr. John Gottman's research on relationships and the "magic ratio." According to Gottman, stable and happy relationships require at least five positive interactions for every negative one during times of conflict. This principle doesn't just apply to marriages or partnerships, it's also crucial in how we approach interactions with children. If we focus excessively on negative moments, as the care providers did with Cooper, we risk overshadowing the many positive interactions and behaviors that build confidence, resilience, and trust.

This imbalance in feedback left Cooper feeling defeated. He struggled to see the value in trying to improve his day if one challenging moment was enough to define it as bad in the eyes of his caregivers. The absence of enough positive reinforcement created a self-fulfilling prophecy, where Cooper started to believe that if his day started poorly, it was destined to remain that way. It was exhausting for Cooper, and for us, as we continuously advocated for a more balanced and fair approach in understanding and responding to his behaviors.

As Cooper's parents, we sought to break this cycle by adopting the "magic ratio" approach in our reflections with him. Each day, we worked to acknowledge and celebrate at least five positive moments or actions for every challenge he faced. For instance, if Cooper had a tough interaction at school, we made it a point to highlight the times he showed kindness, shared with a friend, or worked diligently on a class project. By focusing on these positive moments, we helped Cooper see that his day wasn't defined by a single incident but was instead a mosaic of successes and opportunities for growth.

This shift also aligned with a broader philosophy: life is a mosaic of moments, each offering a new opportunity for learning and growth. The way we perceive and react to these moments significantly shapes our journey, our character, and how we present ourselves to the world. By seeing life through the lens of individual moments, we allow ourselves the space to understand that every experience, whether positive or negative, is a chance to evolve and develop.

A crucial aspect of this perspective is acknowledging that bad moments do not have the power to ruin our entire day or define our identity. It's natural to encounter challenges and setbacks, but these instances do not reflect our entire being or capabilities. Instead, they provide crucial insights into our resilience and adaptability. When faced with difficult situations, the ability to step back, reflect, and learn from these experiences is invaluable. This approach fosters a growth mindset, where obstacles become stepping stones to greater self-awareness and strength.

Furthermore, embracing each moment as an opportunity for growth encourages a more mindful and present way of living. It invites us to be fully engaged with the present, to appreciate the nuances of each experience, and to extract wisdom from even the most mundane occurrences. This mindfulness leads to a more profound appreciation for life, enhancing our interactions and relationships with others. It teaches us to be more compassionate and understanding, both towards ourselves and others, as we recognize that everyone is navigating their own complex array of moments and challenges.

In practice, this philosophy means taking the time to celebrate small victories and learn from missteps without allowing them to overshadow our overall sense of self. It's about recognizing that each day is a fresh canvas, offering endless possibilities to paint a new picture of who we are and who we aspire to be. By viewing life as a series of moments, each with its own lesson and beauty, we cultivate a more resilient, adaptable, and fulfilled existence.

Through the power of positive reinforcement and the understanding that no single moment defines us, Cooper learned to approach life's challenges with greater confidence. By applying the "magic ratio" in our reflections with him, we were able to foster a growth mindset that allowed him to thrive. Each day became a new opportunity to learn, evolve, and show up as the best version of himself, one positive moment at a time.

5. Ɛ

Tшo
One
Ոone

It takes two or more to argue, if one drops out,
there is no arguing

During a family vacation, Cooper found himself
on this exciting adventure. We were driving
along a winding two-lane road through the
lush hills, the kind that offered breathtaking
views of the ocean and the vibrant landscape.
The scenery was so captivating that Big
Dad couldn't resist taking in the sights,

occasionally glancing away from the road to marvel at the beauty around them.

As we navigated the twists and turns, Cooper grew increasingly uneasy. He was acutely aware of the narrow lanes and the potential dangers of driving on such a road. His anxiety peaked when Big Dad, enchanted by the stunning views, took his eyes off the road for a moment too long.

"Big Dad, keep your eyes on the road!" Cooper exclaimed, his voice tinged with worry. He knew the importance of staying focused while driving, especially on a road like this.

Big Dad, slightly startled by Cooper's sudden outburst, said, "Relax, Cooper. I'm just enjoying the view. Look how beautiful it is!"

But Cooper was not comforted. His concern for safety overrode the allure of the scenery. "I know, but I don't want to crash!" he insisted, as his voice rose slightly.

The tension in the car began to build. Cooper, sensing the potential for an argument, remembered the concept we had taught him: Two-One-None. "It takes two or more to argue; if one person drops out, there is no arguing," he repeated to himself, hoping to de-escalate the situation.

After hearing me use the phrase Two-One-None and taking a deep breath, Cooper decided to drop out of the conversation. He turned his attention to the window, silently admiring the view himself. However, Big Dad continued to take his eyes off the road occasionally, not fully grasping why Cooper was so uneasy.

Cooper at Maui Gold Pineapple Farm

Once we arrived at Maui Gold Pineapple, Cooper immediately sought me out. "Mom, can I talk to you?" he asked, his voice still carrying the weight of his earlier uneasiness.

"Of course, buddy," I replied, sensing his distress. We found a quiet spot, and Cooper recounted the events of the drive.

"Big Dad kept looking at the scenery while he was driving, and it made me really nervous.

I told him to keep his eyes on the road, but he didn't understand why I was worried. I used Two-One-None and stopped arguing, but I'm not sure if I handled it right," Cooper explained, his eyes searching me for guidance.

I listened intently before responding. "You did the right thing by expressing your concern, Cooper. It's important to speak up when you feel unsafe. And using Two-One-None to avoid escalating the argument was very mature. Sometimes, people might not understand our worries, but what's important is that you communicated your feelings calmly."

Cooper nodded, feeling a bit reassured but still seeking a solution. "But what should I do if this happens again?"

I smiled gently. "Next time, maybe you can try explaining why it makes you uncomfortable in a calm way, like saying, 'Big Dad, I feel safer when you keep your eyes on the road because it's narrow and curvy.' This way, you're sharing your feelings without it sounding like a command."

Cooper took a deep breath, feeling more at ease with this new approach. "Okay, I'll try that next time."

I hugged him tightly. "I'm proud of you, Cooper. You're learning to handle situations with both assertiveness and patience. That's a great balance to have."

During Cooper's younger years, we discovered a growing challenge: navigating difficult conversations that often escalated into arguments. These situations frequently left Cooper feeling frustrated and us searching for a solution to help him manage these conflicts constructively.

In our quest to find an effective method, we developed a simple yet powerful tool we call

"Two-One-None" This concept was grounded in a straightforward principle: "It takes two or more to argue; if one person drops out, there is no arguing." We explained this idea to Cooper, helping him understand that he had the power to disengage from escalating arguments by simply choosing not to participate.

The first time we introduced "Two-One-None," it was during a particularly heated disagreement over bedtime. As voices began to rise, we gently reminded Cooper of our new mantra. "Remember, Two-One-None," we said. Almost immediately, he paused, took a deep breath, and stepped back from the argument. The tension in the room eased, replaced by a sense of calm and control.

Over time, the mere mention of "Two-One-Non" became a signal for Cooper and the rest of the family to step away from the potential conflict. Whether it was a disagreement over a game with his sister or a misunderstanding with a caregiver, this phrase served as a powerful reminder that anyone can choose to stop the argument before it spiraled out of control. It was empowering for Cooper to realize that he didn't have to engage in every battle, and it provided him with a tangible strategy to manage his emotions and reactions.

As Cooper continues to practice "Two-One-None," we also taught him an essential lesson: sometimes, it takes the bigger, more self-aware person to drop out of a conversation. This awareness means recognizing when a discussion is veering into toxic conflict and choosing to step back rather than getting caught in the emotional swirl. This skill requires a deep understanding of oneself and a commitment to maintaining inner peace over winning or not winning an argument.

We explained to Cooper that walking away from a conflict isn't a sign of weakness but a demonstration of strength and self-control.

By choosing to disengage, he was protecting his emotional well-being and fostering a more harmonious environment. This approach also encouraged Cooper to develop empathy, as he learned to recognize when others might be struggling to manage their emotions.

This tool not only helps Cooper navigate difficult conversations but also taught him an invaluable life lesson about conflict resolution. By learning to step away and not let arguments define his interactions, Cooper developed greater emotional resilience and self-control. The "Two-One-None" method is more than just a phrase; it is a cornerstone of our approach to fostering a peaceful and supportive environment, helping Cooper grow into a more understanding and patient individual. This practice, rooted in self-awareness and empathy, prepares Cooper for a lifetime of healthier, more respectful interactions.

5. F

Player B

When choosing to disengage is winning

I recall the night I took Cooper shopping at the Dollar Tree to reward him for his bravery during his doctor's appointment at the University of Minnesota earlier that afternoon. He had faced a blood draw, which was particularly challenging and frightening for him, yet he managed it with great courage.

At the store, Cooper took his time selecting his reward. He walked up and down the aisles, carefully studying all the options and talking through his choices. After much deliberation, he finally made his selections.

Cooper decided that lane five was where we should check out, so we patiently waited for our turn. When it was our turn, the lady at the checkout greeted us with a "hello". I responded back with a friendly hello, and she then addressed Cooper, saying, "Hello, young man. How are you?"

Cooper immediately looked down and tried to hide behind the checkout counter, feeling overwhelmed. The lady, however, continued to address him. "Hello, young man. How are you? If you do not acknowledge me, I can put these items back on the shelf."

I could sense her frustration growing as she raised her voice, insisting on a response from Cooper. "I'm sure your mom would agree with me that you do not deserve these items if you do not respond to me when I speak to you."

Cooper, clearly distressed, moved closer to me, keeping his gaze fixed on the floor. The lady then reached out and grabbed his shoulder, speaking loudly enough for other customers to hear, "I can touch you. Do you feel me touching you? I am here speaking to you. Do you want to keep these toys, or should I put them back on the shelf?"

At this point, Cooper buried his face into my belly, trying to escape her comments and touch. I hugged him and chose to remain silent. I swiped my card, grabbed the bag, and walked out of the store.

There is a concept we introduced to Cooper to help him navigate the tricky waters of conflict, which we call "Player B." The idea behind this concept stemmed from understanding one's role in managing conflict. In any given conflict, the instigator was referred to as Player A, the person who started the disagreement or confrontation. Player A would often try to provoke a response, baiting the other person into reacting negatively. When that happened, the provoked individual became Player B, falling into the trap and escalating the conflict.

Cooper often found himself in the role of Player B. Whether it was at school, in public, or even at home, there were times when another person, Player A, would trigger him. It could be the lady at the Dollar Tree or his sister pushing his buttons just to get a reaction. Inevitably, Cooper would respond, which often led to him being the one who got into trouble. Unfortunately, Player A's role in initiating the conflict would often go unnoticed, leaving Cooper to face the consequences alone.

We knew we needed to help Cooper understand how to break this cycle. We sat down with him and explained the concept of Player B in a way that he could relate to. "Cooper," we said, "sometimes people will try to provoke you to get a reaction. When they do this, they are being Player A. If you respond negatively, you become Player B, and that's when the trouble starts. But if you recognize what's happening and choose not to respond, you take away their power. You stay out of the game".

To further support him, we coached Cooper on the power of remaining silent in these situations. Our thinking was simple and grounded in a basic principle: no one gets in trouble for remaining silent. By choosing silence, Cooper could avoid escalating the conflict and prevent himself from becoming Player B. We practiced scenarios at home, role-playing different situations where he could be provoked, and discussed how he could respond—or rather, not respond.

Slowly but surely, Cooper started to apply these lessons in real life. He became more aware of when someone was trying to bait him and learned to take a deep breath and walk away instead of reacting. It wasn't always easy, and there were still moments when he slipped into the Player B role, but he was making progress.

One day during soccer practice, Cooper found himself in a potential Player B situation.

Several of his teammates began calling him the R-word, a cruel and derogatory term that stung every time it was repeated. Cooper, trying to stand up for himself, repeatedly asked them to stop, but the taunting only grew louder as more teammates joined in. Two of his friends stepped in, trying to defend him, but their efforts did little to quiet the growing chorus of ridicule.

Amid the chaos, Cooper remembered what we had coached him about Player B and the power of remaining silent. He realized that engaging further would only escalate the situation. Though the insults continued, Cooper chose to disengage. He walked off the field, grabbed his soccer gear, and removed himself from the toxic environment. It was a hard decision for him to make, but he knew it was the best way to protect his emotional well-being.

When Cooper arrived home that evening, tears streamed down his face. The weight of the words and the situation hung heavily on him. We hugged him tightly, allowing him to cry and release the emotions he had been holding in. We assured him that he did the right thing by walking away and praised his courage for handling the situation with such restraint.

"Cooper," we said gently, "what they said was hurtful and wrong, and it says more about them than it does about you. Choosing not to engage was incredibly brave. It shows that you understand your worth and won't let their words define you."

Though the incident was painful, it became a teachable moment. We talked about the importance of standing up for oneself, but also recognizing when it's time to step away to avoid further harm. Cooper learned that sometimes, walking away is the strongest action you can take, even when it feels unfair or unresolved.

As the days went on, Cooper processed the experience with our support. We encouraged him to focus on the people who cared about him and reminded him of the strength it took to prioritize his well-being. This experience, while challenging, reinforced his ability to navigate conflicts with dignity and self-respect, proving once again that even in difficult moments, he was growing into a resilient and thoughtful young man.

The concept of Player B, coupled with the strategy of remaining silent, became invaluable tools for Cooper, helping him to navigate conflicts with greater self-control and awareness. It taught him that while he couldn't always control how others behaved, he could control his own reactions. This lesson not only helped him avoid unnecessary trouble but also fostered a sense of empowerment and resilience that will serve him well throughout his life.

5. G

Scaled Response

Small problem = Small response
Big Problem = Big Response

One sunny afternoon in second grade, Cooper was lining up with his classmates after lunch, ready to return to the classroom. The line was usually a bustling place, with kids chatting and jostling for position. Cooper, who always tried his best to follow the rules, stood quietly, waiting for the teacher to lead them back.

As the teacher was organizing the line, she noticed two girls running and called out to them, asking them to stop and join the line properly. Cooper, seeing this, decided to help the teacher enforce the rule. He stepped out of line and, with a stern expression, repeated the teacher's instructions to the girls.

"Hey, you need to stop running and get in line!" Cooper said, his voice louder than usual.

The girls, startled by Cooper's tone, stopped immediately but looked a bit confused and slightly scared. They hadn't expected their classmate to reprimand them so forcefully. The teacher, noticing the situation, quickly intervened.

"Thank you, Cooper, but it's okay. I've got it from here," she said gently, guiding him back into line. She smiled at him, appreciating his intention to help but recognizing that his response needed some adjustment.

Later that day, the teacher took Cooper aside for a quiet chat. "Cooper," she began, "I appreciate that you want to help and that you're following the rules. But sometimes, it's important to let the teacher handle these situations. When you speak to your classmates, it's good to be firm but also kind. Do you understand?"

Cooper nodded, trying to process what she was saying. He realized that while his intention was to assist, his approach might have been too harsh. The teacher continued, "It's all about the right response for the right situation. When someone is breaking a rule, it's my job to handle it. You can help by being a good example and reminding them gently if needed."

We noticed that Cooper's reactions were often tied to his emotions, which he didn't fully understand. When a problem arose, whether big or small, his emotions would surge, leaving him confused and overwhelmed. He didn't know why he felt so intensely, which made it hard for him to connect his feelings to an appropriate response.

Cooper donating his sensory wheelies to Ms Partington at CherryView Elementary School

Recognizing this challenge, Ms. Partington, Cooper's elementary teacher, stepped in to help him learn the scaled response model. She worked closely with Cooper, using a visual chart that depicted different levels of problems and corresponding reactions. Through consistent practice and gentle guidance, Ms. Partington taught Cooper to identify the severity of an issue and choose an appropriate response.

We also taught him to identify his emotions and understand why he felt the way he did. We practiced this through role-playing and discussions, helping him to articulate his feelings and recognize when they were disproportionate to the situation at hand. Over time, Cooper began to see the connection between his emotions and his responses, learning to temper his reactions to better fit the problems he faces.

Small problem = Small response.
Big problem = Big response.

Gradually, we saw improvements. Cooper started to pause and think before reacting, assessing the scale of the problem and choosing a more measured response. He became more aware of his emotions and better equipped to handle them. This newfound ability to scale his reactions not only helped him manage his emotions more effectively but also allowed him to show up as his best self in challenging situations.

In the end, Cooper learned that understanding and managing his emotions was key to navigating life's ups and downs. By scaling his reactions to match the problems he faced, he was able to maintain a sense of control and respond more appropriately, paving the way for greater emotional resilience and personal growth.

6.

Thriving

Sustaining success with the skills to navigate life

I'll never forget the day Cooper, at just seven years old, had a therapy session with Ms. Abby, who suggested I step outside the room to help him learn that he could feel safe even without me right there beside him. Cooper, however, had a very different opinion on the matter. Without hesitation, he grabbed the table, flipped it over, and yelled "Bitches!" at the top of his lungs. Ms. Abby remained calm, trying to soothe him, but after a few minutes, she opened the door, looked at me, and simply said, "Well, that was an experience." We both burst into laughter, it was chaotic, yes, but it was also just another step in the journey.

Looking back, that moment feels like a lifetime ago. Today, Cooper is a completely different person, engaged, independent, and thriving in ways we once only dreamed about. But this transformation didn't happen by accident. It was grounded in the structured, intentional approach of the carefully designed playbook of tools, which became the foundation of our family's journey.

Through observation, trial and error, constant adjustments, and countless retries, we created these tools, giving us, as parents, the structure and clarity we so desperately needed amid the disorder. They brought clarity to the chaos and showed us that Cooper's success was intrinsically tied to the support we provided and the strategies we taught him to use. It was through this framework that we realized our role wasn't just about managing behaviors, but about equipping Cooper with the skills to navigate the world confidently.

The tools empowered us to turn overwhelming challenges into manageable milestones. With each strategy, we saw Cooper make strides, not just academically but in his ability to regulate emotions, advocate for himself, and connect with others. The tools weren't merely instructions; they became life skills, empowering Cooper to engage with the world around him in meaningful ways.

Through structured techniques, we learned to anticipate and diffuse emotional outbursts, turning what once felt like insurmountable obstacles into opportunities for growth. We began to see patterns, understand triggers, and most importantly, teach Cooper how to manage them himself. These tools became our compass, helping us steer through uncharted territories with confidence and hope.

For Cooper, the results speak volumes. The same child who once struggled to adapt is now excelling in school, taking initiative, and even asking for more challenging school work. His participation in activities like the high school soccer team, esports, and Civil Air Patrol highlights his growing independence and engagement. His transformation has been nothing short of inspiring.

Together, these tools form a comprehensive framework that guides through the complexities of social interactions, emotional regulation, and effective communication. They are not just strategies but life skills that empower Cooper to navigate his world with more confidence and resilience. And for us, as parents, they've been a lifeline, bringing order in the disorder and providing a roadmap to help Cooper reach his fullest potential. This foundation sets the stage for a future where he can continue to grow and thrive, equipped with the skills and confidence to take on whatever comes his way.

7.

Shaped by the Storms

The foundation upon which Cooper's strength, determination, and trust in God were built

You never forget the sound of your child asking why God made him the way he is, especially when it is laced with heartbreak.

It was one of those quiet, chilly evenings as Cooper and I drove home from yet another specialist appointment. The hum of the tires on the road filled the silence between us. He stared out the window, his face catching the light of passing streetlamps, lost in thought. I could tell something was stirring deep inside him. Then, suddenly, he spoke. His voice cut through the stillness like a blade.

"Why did God make me the way I am?" he asked, filled with frustration and pain.

I glanced at him, my heart aching. His brows were furrowed, his eyes searching for something, answers maybe, or reassurance I wasn't sure I could give. Before I could respond, he added with a crack in his voice, "Why did He let me get beat up like that? What's the point of having faith in God if this is how my life is going to be?"

The rawness of his words took the air from my lungs. I tightened my grip on the steering wheel, steadying myself and trying to find words that could both comfort and honor the weight of his questions. Cooper had always been a deep thinker, but this question was a window into the profound struggle he was grappling with, a battle of faith and the painful reality of what he had endured. I knew I had to tread carefully, offering him honesty without diminishing his pain.

"Cooper," I began softly, my voice carrying both love and caution, "that's a really big question, and it's okay to feel the way you do. What happened to you wasn't fair. It wasn't right, and it's something no one should ever have to go through."

He didn't respond, but I could tell he was listening. I continued, "I don't know why God allowed that to happen, and I don't know why you've had to face so many challenges. But what I do know is that God didn't create you to suffer. He created you with purpose, even if that purpose isn't clear yet."

Cooper turned slightly toward me, skepticism etched into his expression. "What purpose? To be someone other people hurt? To just... deal with it?"

"No," I said, my voice firmer now. "Your purpose isn't to be hurt. But I believe that sometimes the hardest moments give us a chance to uncover a strength we never knew we had. Maybe it's not about asking why God let this happen but about what you'll do with it now. And Cooper, you've already shown more courage than most people ever do in a lifetime."

The car grew quiet again, but this time, the silence was different. He was processing, not retreating. I took a deep breath and added, "Faith isn't about everything being perfect. It's about trusting that even when life feels unfair or impossible, God hasn't walked away. He's in the people who've helped you, in the strength that's kept you going, and in the fact that you're still here, still trying, still growing."

As we pulled into the driveway, I reached over and rested my hand on his hand. "It's okay to have questions. It's okay to be angry. God can handle that. And no matter what, I'm here to walk with you through all of it."

That night, I didn't have all the answers. I still don't. But in that moment, I witnessed a young boy wrestle with some of life's deepest questions. His willingness to confront them head-on showed me just how strong his spirit truly is. Even in darkness, light has a way of breaking through.

The incident left Cooper with more than just physical scars. The emotional wounds ran deep. But instead of allowing bitterness to take root, he leaned into the tools that had sustained him through previous challenges: mindfulness, emotional regulation, and conflict resolution. Those tools helped him stay calm during the attack and later helped him process what came after.

Months later, the legal process began to unfold. It was long and exhausting, marked by several court appearances that pulled at all of our nerves. Finally, after what felt like an eternity, the boy who had attacked Cooper was convicted of third-degree felony assault.

Sitting in that courtroom on the day of the conviction, Cooper experienced something hard to explain. It was not relief, and it was not triumph. It was a sobering and quiet moment of accountability. It was the realization that what happened to him mattered beyond just our family's experience.

Cooper felt steadiness. Validation. Watching the system acknowledge the harm he had suffered gave him a sense of resolution. It did not undo the damage, but it helped him begin to move forward.

Accountability, he realized, is not about revenge. It is about recognition. Sitting in court, he saw that actions have consequences and that harm cannot go unanswered. That moment did not erase the pain, but it gave structure to it. It turned chaos into clarity. And in that clarity, Cooper found a new layer of strength.

He did not let that chapter define him. He did not see himself as broken or defined by what someone else had done. He chose to keep growing. He became a young man marked not by trauma, but by perseverance and grace.

That resilience did not form in isolation. It was nurtured by an incredible team of therapists, educators, advocates, and family members who stood with us every step of the way. Their presence reminded Cooper that pain may shape us, but it does not have to break us.

His journey is a powerful reminder that growth is still possible even in the middle of life's storms. Even when faith feels fragile, it can be rebuilt. Even when circumstances feel overwhelming, we are never beyond hope.

Cooper's story is not just about hardship. It is about grit, healing, and unwavering perseverance. It shows the kind of faith that walks through suffering instead of around it and believes that there is still something good ahead.

So if you or someone you love is feeling overwhelmed, take heart. The questions might be heavy. The nights might be long. The road ahead might feel impossible. But know this: you are not alone.

And like Cooper, you have within you a strength greater than the obstacles before you. Even when everything feels uncertain, there is hope in each step forward.

Lean into your faith. Lean on the people who lift you up. And when life knocks you down, remember that resilience is not just about getting back up. It is about rising stronger, with deeper understanding and greater *Response-ABILITY*, the ability to respond with intention, not just react. It is about finding peace in the middle of chaos and learning to use every challenge as a stepping stone for growth.

Resilience takes root in connection. It grows when we show up for one another with steady presence and unwavering compassion. When we consistently show up for the children in our lives, with listening ears, open hearts, and calm reassurance, we help them build the foundation for something lasting. We give them room to feel, the courage to ask hard questions, and the confidence to respond to life rather than be overwhelmed by it.

This is the quiet but powerful work of shaping a life. We are not called to clear every obstacle from their path. We are called to walk it with them. To model how to face difficulty with grace and grit. To offer steadiness in the uncertainty. And to reflect back to them the truth of who they are when the world tries to make them forget.

Wherever you are in this journey, as a parent, caregiver, educator, mentor, or friend, please remember: your presence matters more than you may ever know.

You do not need to be perfect. You only need to be present.

Keep showing up. Keep choosing connection. Keep believing that what you offer, even in the smallest of moments, can help unlock strength, healing, and possibility in the life of a child.

Because when we show up with intention, we give them the ability to respond with courage.

And that can change everything.

Appendix

The below outline provides a structured outline for parents and caregivers to organize and share key information about their child. It is designed to help others, such as educators, therapists, and caregivers, better understand the child's unique strengths, needs, and strategies for effective support. By presenting the information in a clear, concise, and positive manner, this template fosters collaboration and ensures a more tailored, supportive approach to the child's growth and development.

1. Title Slide
- Title of the presentation
- Presenter's name (Parent's name)
- Date of presentation

2. Introduction
- Brief introduction about the purpose
- A short personal introduction about the child (name, age, interests)

3. Understanding Autism Spectrum Disorder
- Definition of Autism Spectrum Disorder (ASD)
- Common characteristics of ASD
- Emphasize the spectrum nature of autism

4. Our Child's Autism Diagnosis
- Brief story of how and when the diagnosis was made
- Any key medical professionals or therapists involved

5. Daily Life and Routines
- Overview of the child's daily schedule
- Importance of routines and structure for the child
- Strategies used at home to support these routines

6. Communication Preferences and Challenges
- How the child communicates (verbal, non-verbal, AAC devices, etc.)
- Understanding and interpreting the child's communication cues
- Challenges in communication and how to address them

7. Social Interaction and Behavior
- Child's approach to social interaction
- Any specific social challenges (e.g., understanding social cues)
- Preferred ways of socializing and engaging with others

8. Sensory Sensitivities and Accommodations
- Specific sensory sensitivities (sounds, lights, textures, etc.)
- How these sensitivities impact daily life
- Accommodations and strategies that help

9. Strengths and Interests
- Highlight the child's strengths and talents
- Discuss the child's interests and how they engage with them
- How these strengths and interests are incorporated into learning and development

10. Educational and Behavioral Support Needs
- Overview of the child's educational setting and any supports in place
- Behavioral challenges and effective strategies
- How teachers and caregivers can provide support in educational settings

11. Partnerships with Professionals

- Overview of the professionals involved in the child's care (therapists, educators, medical professionals)
- How these partnerships contribute to the child's development
- Importance of consistent communication between home and school/therapy settings

12. Tips for Successful Interaction

- Practical tips for interacting with the child
- How to respond to difficult situations or behaviors
- Encouraging positive interactions and experiences

13. Q&A Session

- Allow time for questions and answers
- Provide additional resources if available (websites, books, support groups, youtube videos)

14. Acknowledgements
- Thank attendees for their time and interest
- Acknowledge any professionals or organizations that have been particularly helpful

15. Appendix
- Include any additional resources or references
- Contact information for relevant local support services and organizations

One Thing About Me Worksheet

Item 2

Use this resource as an opportunity for your child to share their perspective and express how they see themselves. Encourage them to fill it out in their own words, and take the time to explore their responses together. Use the insights gained as a valuable tool to better understand and support them in meaningful and personalized ways.

One Thing About Me Worksheet

What five words best describe you?

_____   _____

_____   _____

_____

Draw a picture of yourself

Complete the following statement

One thing you need to know about me is...

_____

Pillars of Action

Item 3

The Pillars of Actions template, offers a structured way to apply the Advocate-Motivate-Participate framework. This template includes practical tools for organizing goals, strategies, and progress tracking. It helps caregivers identify specific learning goals, tools for support, mindset shifts, and sensory/environmental adjustments. The progress check-ins allow for regular evaluation, ensuring that strategies remain tailored and effective for the individual's needs.

Advocate

Knowledge / Support
What do I need to know to be a proactive advocate?

What is my advocacy goal?

What experts can I learn from?

Acceptance / Awareness
What tool(s) are needed to advocate?

What methods will be used to advocate?

Who will assist in advocacy?

Motivate

Mindset / Attitude
What are the fixed mindset/attitudes?

_____

_____

What default setting exist?

_____

_____

What do "Go" actions look like?

_____

_____

Goal(s) / Reward(s)
What do we want to see more of? / What do we not want to see any of?
How do we reward progress?
How often will we check progress?

Goal(s)	Reward(s)	Progress Check-In

Participate

Environment / Sensory Considerations
What environments are challenging to be in?

What sensory processing difficulties exist?

What supports can be provided to encourage participation?

Trigger(s) / Response(s)
What are emotional / behavioral triggers?
What do repsonses look like?
How big is the impact?

Triggers	Response	Level of Impact
		Low / Medium / High
		Low / Medium / High
		Low / Medium / High
		Low / Medium / High
		Low / Medium / High
		Low / Medium / High
		Low / Medium / High

Enhance Core Competencies

Item 4

A capability model is a detailed graphical representation designed to systematically outline the progression and enhancement of specific skills, focusing particularly on the domains of social interaction, emotional intelligence, effective communication, and self-management abilities.

This chart serves as a strategic tool for identifying and developing these key competencies in a structured and measurable way.

Make time each year to identify the capabilities you want to prioritize and focus on and then check on the progress made monthly and quarterly.

Social (SQ) | Emotional (EQ) | Communication (CQ)

Social (SQ)		Emotional (EQ)		Communication (CQ)	
Social Awareness	Relationship Management	Emotional Awareness	Emotional Management	Intrapersonal	Interpersonal
Social Standards/ Principles	Interpersonal Skills	Emotional Identification	Response Management	Speech Development	Advocacy Management
Situational Awareness	Conflict Management	Emotional Regulation	Choice Management	Self-Reflection Management	Response Management
Situational Management	Skill Management	Classification Management	Action Management	Response Methods	Eye Contact Management
Bias Management	Decision Making	Trigger Points	Maturity Management	Self Talk	Listening Skills
Impact Management	Communication Management	Temperament	Impulse Management	Perception Management	Verbal/ Non-Verbal Management
Trigger Management	Trust Building			Expectation Management	Feedback Management

Self

Self Awareness				Self Management		
Diagnosis Awareness	Self-Worth	Self-Confidence	Trigger Points	Default Settings	Mindset Management	Outcomes Management
Environmental Management	Value Identification Management	Sensory Awareness		Guiding Principles	Coping Tool Management	Stress Management

1. Mark current and desired abilities on the maturity line for each core competency

2. Select one to two core competencies as priority based on need and/or gap between current & desired ability

3. Plot prioritized competencies based on level of motivation and skill

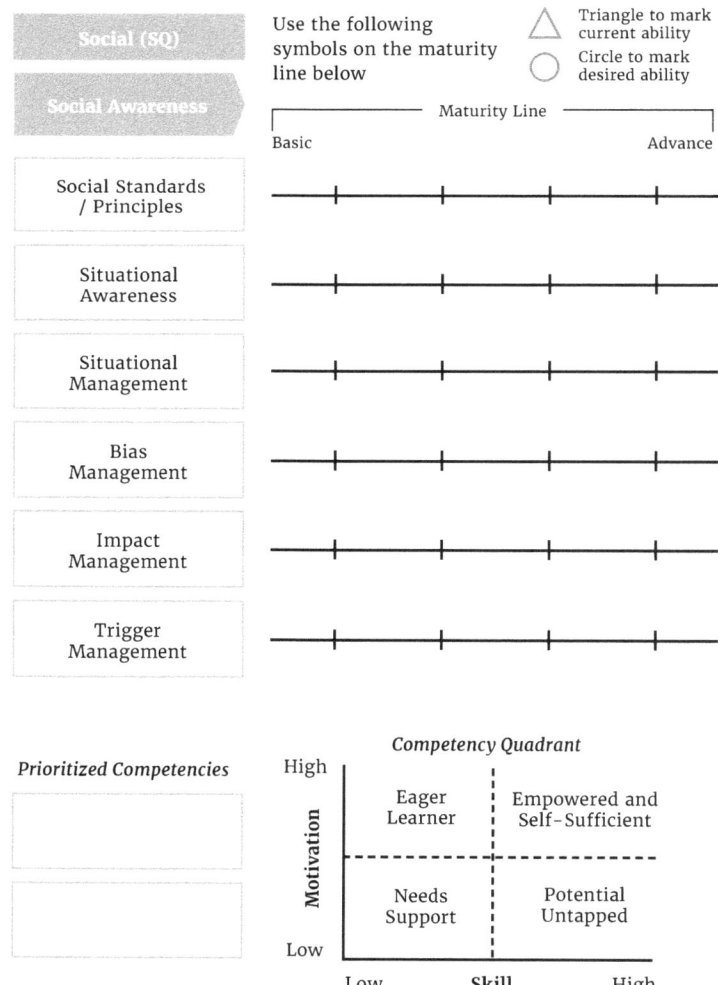

1. Mark current and desired abilities on the maturity line for each core competency

2. Select one to two core competencies as priority based on need and/or gap between current & desired ability

3. Plot prioritized competencies based on level of motivation and skill

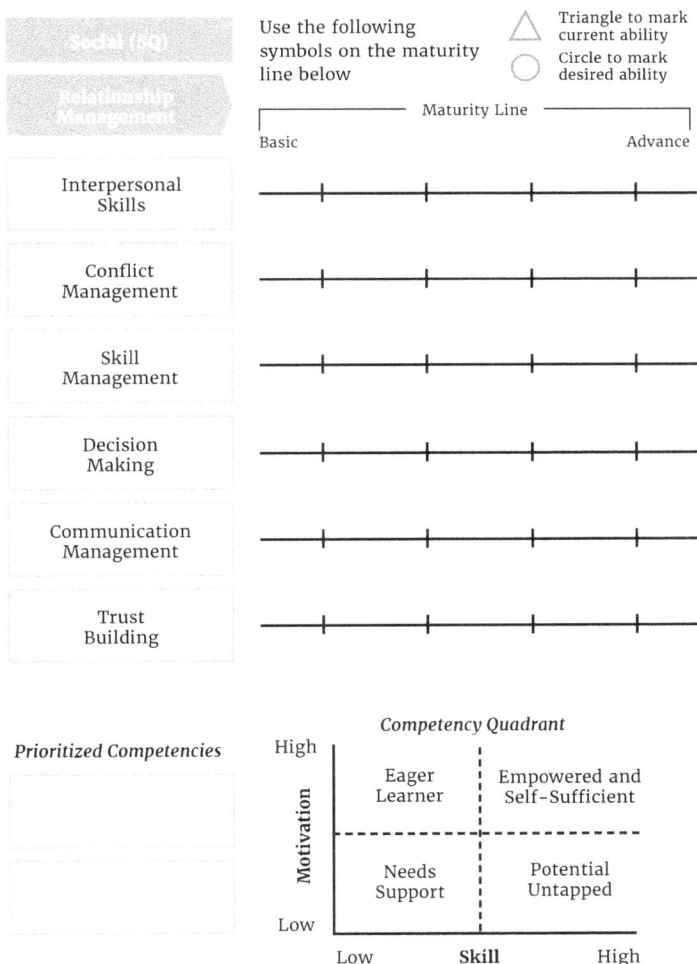

Social (SQ)

Relationship Management

Use the following symbols on the maturity line below

△ Triangle to mark current ability
○ Circle to mark desired ability

Maturity Line

Basic   Advance

Interpersonal Skills

Conflict Management

Skill Management

Decision Making

Communication Management

Trust Building

Prioritized Competencies

Competency Quadrant

High

Motivation

Eager Learner | Empowered and Self-Sufficient

Needs Support | Potential Untapped

Low

Low   Skill   High

1. Mark current and desired abilities on the maturity line for each core competency

2. Select one to two core competencies as priority based on need and/or gap between current & desired ability

3. Plot prioritized competencies based on level of motivation and skill

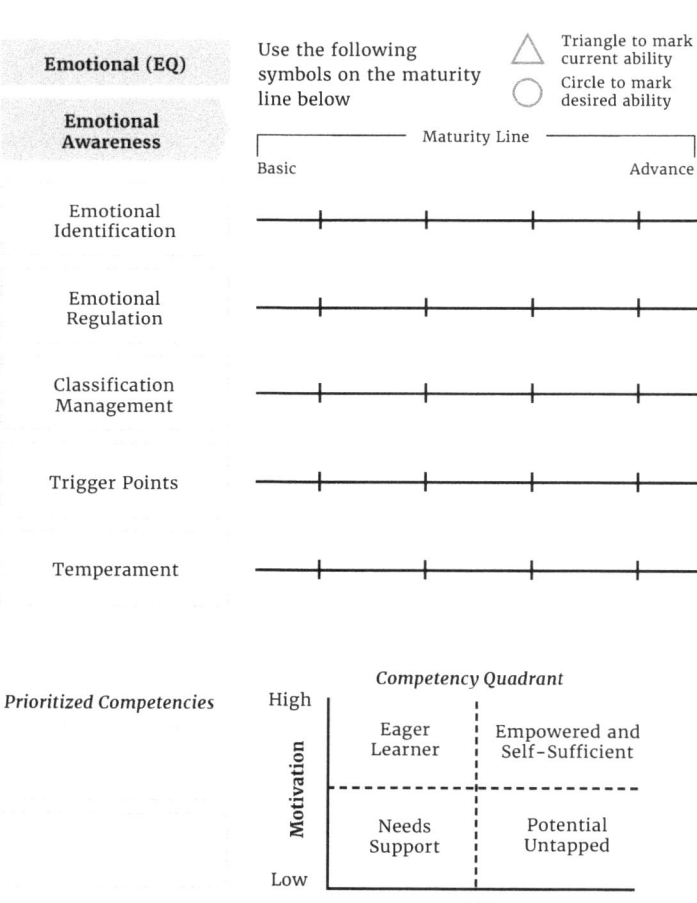

Emotional (EQ)

Emotional Awareness

Use the following symbols on the maturity line below

△ Triangle to mark current ability

○ Circle to mark desired ability

Maturity Line

Basic   Advance

Emotional Identification

Emotional Regulation

Classification Management

Trigger Points

Temperament

Prioritized Competencies

Competency Quadrant

	Low Skill	High Skill
High Motivation	Eager Learner	Empowered and Self-Sufficient
Low Motivation	Needs Support	Potential Untapped

Low   Skill   High

1. Mark current and desired abilities on the maturity line for each core competency

2. Select one to two core competencies as priority based on need and/or gap between current & desired ability

3. Plot prioritized competencies based on level of motivation and skill

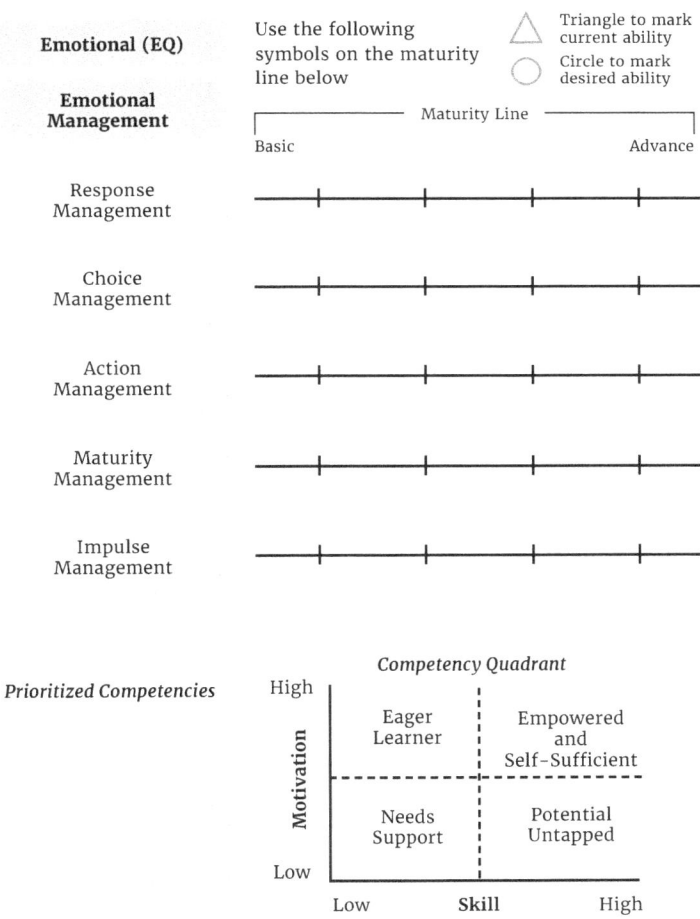

175

1. Mark current and desired abilities on the maturity line for each core competency

2. Select one to two core competencies as priority based on need and/or gap between current & desired ability

3. Plot prioritized competencies based on level of motivation and skill

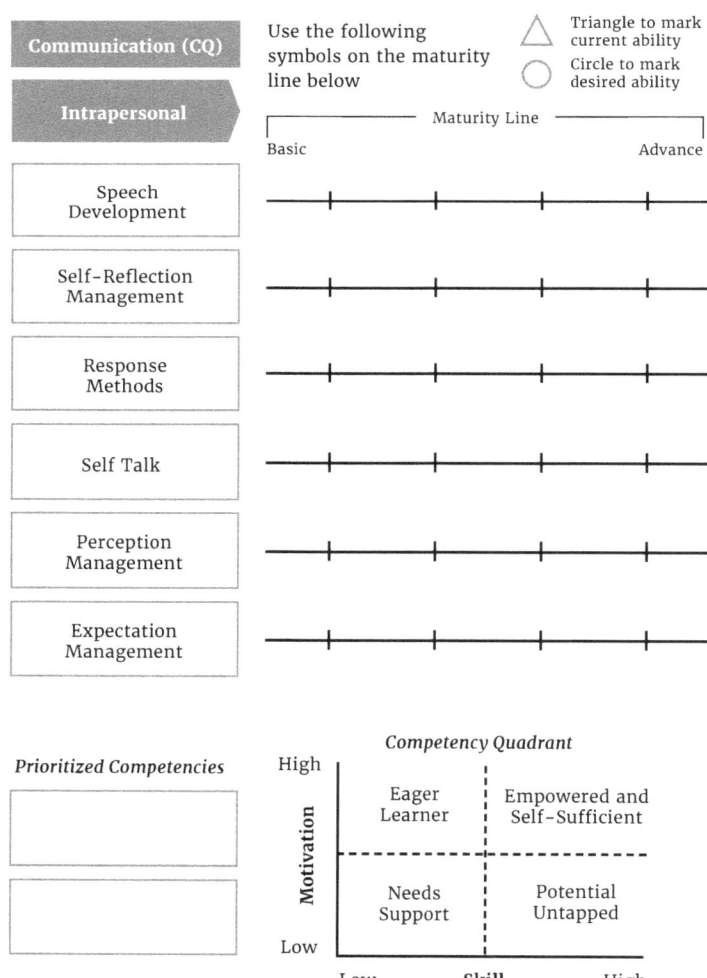

1. Mark current and desired abilities on the maturity line for each core competency

2. Select one to two core competencies as priority based on need and/or gap between current & desired ability

3. Plot prioritized competencies based on level of motivation and skill

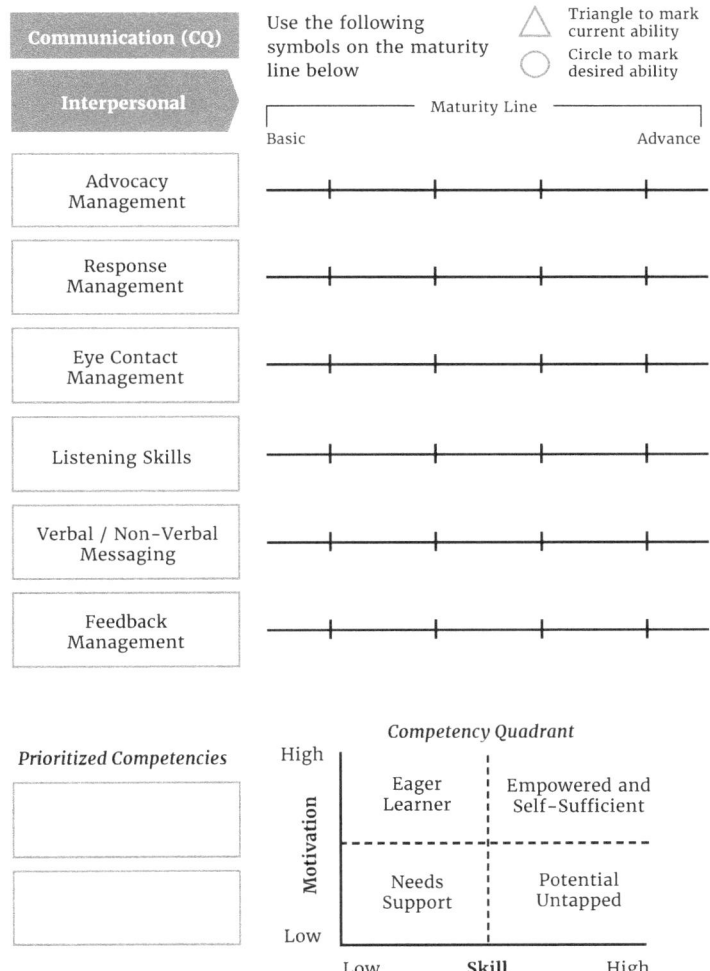

1. Mark current and desired abilities on the maturity line for each core competency

2. Select one to two core competencies as priority based on need and/or gap between current & desired ability

3. Plot prioritized competencies based on level of motivation and skill

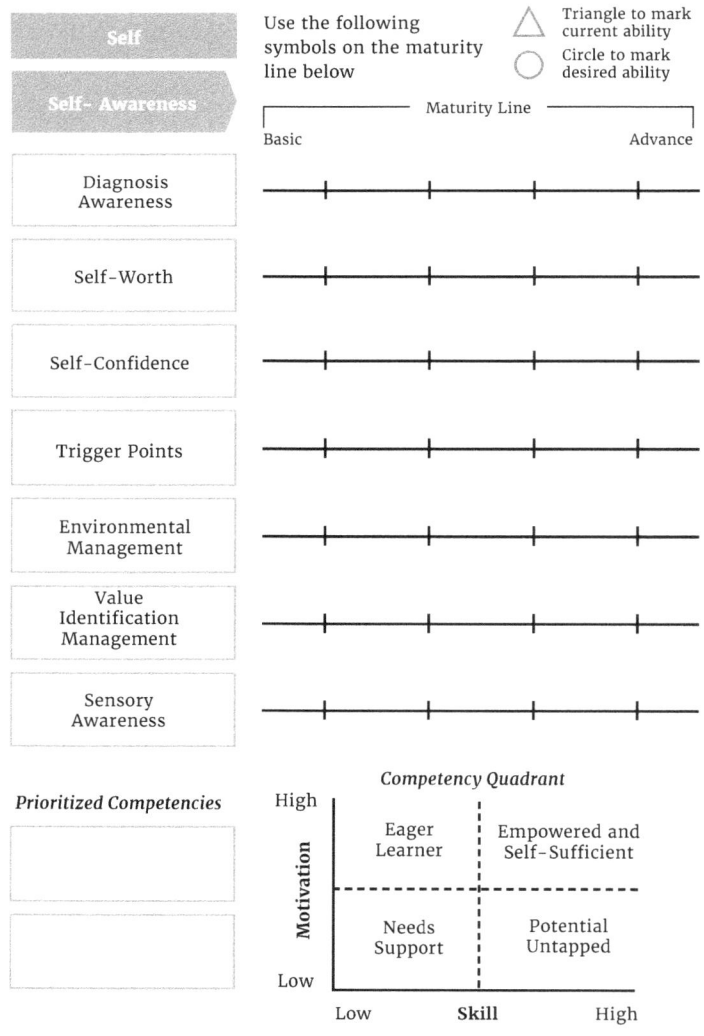

Self

Self- Awareness

Use the following symbols on the maturity line below

△ Triangle to mark current ability

○ Circle to mark desired ability

┌──────── Maturity Line ────────┐

Basic   Advance

Diagnosis Awareness

Self-Worth

Self-Confidence

Trigger Points

Environmental Management

Value Identification Management

Sensory Awareness

Prioritized Competencies

Competency Quadrant

High

Motivation

| | Eager Learner | Empowered and Self-Sufficient |
| Needs Support | Potential Untapped |

Low

Low   **Skill**   High

1. Mark current and desired abilities on the maturity line for each core competency

2. Select one to two core competencies as priority based on need and/or gap between current & desired ability

3. Plot prioritized competencies based on level of motivation and skill

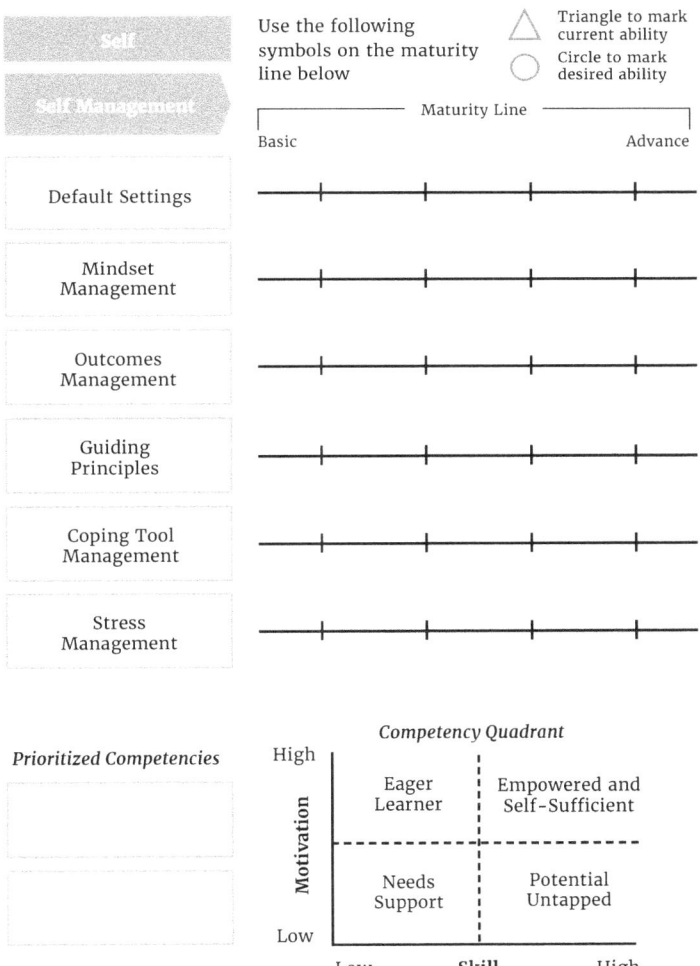

Self

Self Management

Use the following symbols on the maturity line below

△ Triangle to mark current ability

○ Circle to mark desired ability

Maturity Line

Basic | Advance

Default Settings	
Mindset Management	
Outcomes Management	
Guiding Principles	
Coping Tool Management	
Stress Management	

Prioritized Competencies

Competency Quadrant

Motivation: High / Low

Skill: Low / High

Eager Learner | Empowered and Self-Sufficient

Needs Support | Potential Untapped

1. Place the prioritized core competencies from the different categories on the prior pages here
2. Regularly reasses and adjust prioritized competencies as the individual grows or face challenges

Social (SQ)	Emotional (EQ)
Social Awareness	**Emotional Awareness**
Relationship Management	**Emotional Management**

Communication (CQ)	Self
Intrapersonal	**Self-Awareness**
Interpersonal	**Self Management**

1. Take all the Prioritized Core Competencies from the various categories and place them in the quadrant that aligns with their motivation and skills
2. Seeing all the competencies in the quadrant will give a holistic perspective on what to focus on
3. Determine which of the competencies you will focus on
4. Regularly reassess and adjust placements as the individual grows or faces challenges.

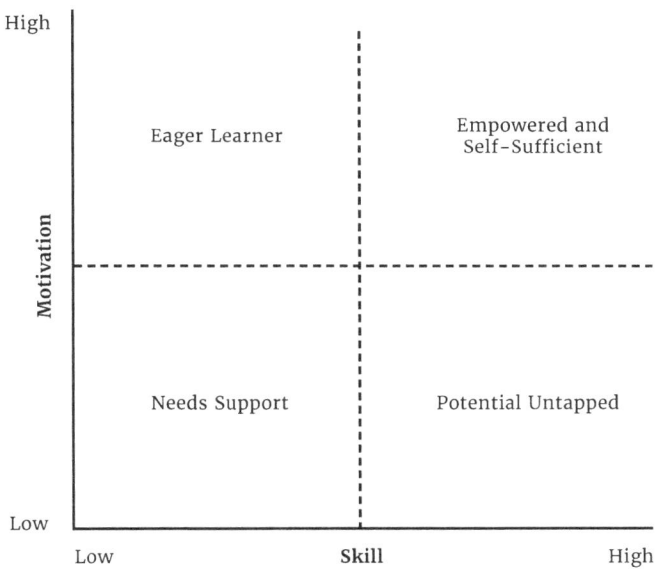

Competency Quadrant

Empowered and Self-Sufficient: Empower autonomy and provide opportunities to lead

Eager Learner: Focus on skill-building through coaching, training, and ecouragement

Potential Untapped: Explore inherent motivators and set meaningful challenges

Needs Support: Start with foundational support, small wins, and external motivation to build confidence

Functions of Behavior Log

1. Take a moment to reflect on common situations that repeatedly occur to identify the function of behavior i.e. Attention seeking, Avoidance, Tangible, Sensory

2. Make sure the response is aligned to the function of behavior to effectively address the behavior and improve the individual's response to situations

Situation	Trigger(s)	Behavior(s)	Function of Behavior	Response	Impact	Future Adjustment(s)